THE JOY OF MOVEMENT

THE JOY OF MOVEMENT

Lesson Plans and Large-Motor Activities for Preschoolers

by Mary Lynn Hafner, PT, DPT

Redleaf Press®
www.redleafpress.org
800-423-8309

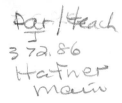

To the devoted preschool teachers who bring joy to children

Published by Redleaf Press
10 Yorkton Court
St. Paul, MN 55117
www.redleafpress.org

First edition 2018
Cover design by Charles Rue Woods
Cover photographs by iStock.com/Fat Camera; gbh007; Global Stock;
Simarik; Lisa Valder; kdshutterman
Interior design by Erin Kirk New
Typeset in Sentinel and Futura
Printed in the United States of America
25 24 23 22 21 20 19 18   1 2 3 4 5 6 7 8

ISBN 978-1-60554-642-1

CIP data is on file with the Library of Congress.

Printed on acid-free paper

CONTENTS

ACKNOWLEDGMENTS

A special shout-out to the teachers, children, and community at Fort Hunt Preschool in Alexandria, Virginia: without them this book would not have been possible.

Thank you to my family, especially Gaby, Gavin, Nadia, and Anya, who honored the *Working* sign when it was on my office door, and who inspire me every day. Thanks to my friend Media C. for your steadfast support, and thanks also to Audrey J., who reinforced my point of view with her journalistic savvy.

You never know what you are going to do next time!

INTRODUCTION
Is This Developmentally Appropriate?

Are you frustrated with your preschool lesson plans? Tired of spending hours looking for new ideas on preschool blogs?

You might be a parent looking for unique activities for a birthday party or playdate. Perhaps you're a grandparent who wants to connect with your grandchildren.

A child care provider wants to stand out from other child care centers. Do you need to evaluate the activities you provide? Are you providing motor control experiences that target developmental milestones?

If you said yes to any of these questions, read on.

In 2010 I became the movement teacher at a play-based, cooperative preschool program my twin daughters attended. The preschool relied on parent and family volunteer hours to assist paid staff in the education of children two to six years old. There was an opening for the position, and I needed to accumulate volunteer hours. It was a good match.

But let's back up a little. This is why I agreed to the position: on one of my scheduled classroom days, my twins' class of three-year-olds went to a large room we affectionately called the "rainbow room." It had a stained-glass window high up on the rear wall, which cast beautiful light of all colors onto the floor when the sun shone through the window. I loved this room!

The volunteer movement teacher, parent of a former student, instructed my daughters' class to play a "chase-the-octopus" game. My girls not only didn't understand the complex rules but also didn't want to be "eaten" by the octopus or tagged by other children. It was too scary for them. They hovered next to my legs the whole time.

For the next game, they were asked to throw beanbags at a target. Guess what the target was? That big ol' stained-glass window, about twenty feet up

the wall. That's a pretty impossible and discouraging task for three-feet-tall children.

OK, I thought, this could be better. I wasn't bashing this amazing volunteer who was donating her valuable time to our children. Yet I was taken aback by how developmentally inappropriate the activities were.

As a parent, I just wanted to build my children's self-esteem and give them a sense of "I can do this!" I wanted them to feel safe trying without feeling they had to compete. When the movement teacher position opened, I volunteered to teach a few classes. I figured I could accumulate my required volunteer hours and stop complaining inwardly about the class. Those few classes eventually turned into a paid position, which continued after my twins graduated from preschool.

A Physical Therapist's Perspective

My experience illustrates the fact that there are no requirements for teaching physical education in early education. Plus, it can be hard to find qualified teachers. That said, some programs are working toward incorporating developmentally appropriate exercise in preschool. Prominent organizations support this effort with position statements on movement education. In addition, research supports the positive effects of early movement education on child development.

As a licensed physical therapist (PT) with an undergraduate and doctoral degree in physical therapy (DPT), I have spent more than twenty-one years studying and working with muscles, motor development, physical assessment, and treatment planning with various age groups in many settings. I have four children. I have also observed and participated in countless movement classes with my children. All of this influenced the format of the movement lesson plans in this book.

A physical therapist is a specialist in neuromuscular development, movement, and exercise. Understanding motor development and body systems helps us think about ways to maximize potential movement patterns for the developing preschooler. A physical therapist is an expert on *the movement system*. The vision statement from the American Physical Therapy Association (APTA) says that the physical therapy profession is "transforming society by optimizing movement to improve the human experience" (APTA 2013). The APTA (accessed 2018) also says that "physical therapists provide a unique perspective on purposeful, precise, and efficient movement across the lifespan based upon the synthesis of their distinctive knowledge of the movement system and expertise in mobility and locomotion."

Since I work as a PT primarily with adults, I rarely label or diagnose my preschool students. I like to think this allows me to be less intimidating to the families I serve, because my only goal is to provide a fun learning environment that promotes and enhances children's motor development.

I created the lessons and games in this book based on my experiences not only as a parent but also as a physical therapist. I used published research to validate and enhance the lessons. Then, most importantly, all lessons were child tested.

When I started planning my classes, I would spend hours scouring the internet, looking for reliable resources and ideas. (Pinterest was and is the easiest source and is especially helpful because it provides pictures and captions.) Yet I still struggled to find a source that had everything I needed.

You won't have to go through that, thanks to my previous preschool director in Alexandria, Virginia. She asked me to leave behind some of my lesson plans for the new movement teacher before I relocated to Washington State.

Many edits later, those lesson plans have evolved into what you hold in your hands. This book practically wrote itself during the five years I taught preschool movement classes in Alexandria, and includes lessons that I teach for a drop-in movement class with preschoolers at my local YMCA.

The lessons are simple and don't use an overwhelming amount of jargon, so you can use the ideas right away. Let them be a source of inspiration for your own brainstorming. The lessons in this book are easy to implement, and the materials they incorporate are affordable.

Movement Class Goals

Your movement class goals are to

- offer opportunities for visual (see), auditory (hear), tactile (touch), and motor (move) learning;

- build a foundation of motor skills through fun and activity;

- provide class with a flexible structure; and emphasize personal development instead of competition.

PART I
The Foundation of Movement

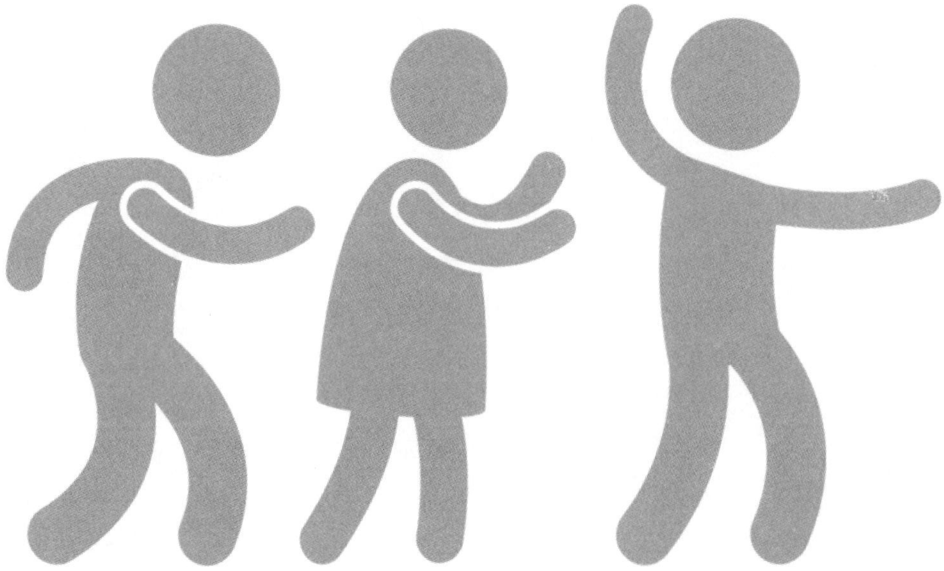

CHAPTER 1
The Lesson Plans

This book contains thirty-six complete lesson plans that are geared toward children three to six years old. They can be used for groups of three to sixteen children, with each lesson lasting an average of thirty to forty minutes.

Each lesson can easily be lengthened or shortened to serve your needs. These lessons are perfect for preschool-specialty physical education teachers and for preschool teachers who want to enhance their everyday curriculum with additional active movement.

Does your class include children who have unclear body boundaries because they crave sensory input and have limited awareness of their personal space? Keep on reading: these children would benefit from this book's lessons that provide experience in using "big-body" movements successfully. The lessons here will enhance your ability to use movement to create focus for all students in your class and will enrich any educational classroom activity.

Please make these lessons your own. If you dislike certain preschool songs or activities, just don't do them. Your students or children will know you dislike them. They will not buy into the activity.

Sometimes you will have to spend more time on an activity that your students love or less time on a skill they are struggling with. You will find that my selection of activities leans toward things I enjoy doing while attempting to create a variety of experiences for the students.

I am not reinventing the wheel. This is my spin on a movement class for preschoolers. I remember patting myself on the back for being creative with an idea that I had incorporated into a lesson. I had placed hand-shaped, laminated pieces of colored paper on a long wall in the rainbow room. The children then lined up and tapped or gently hit the hands by reaching up or down the wall as they walked. The motor goal was to encourage upper-body strengthening and shoulder strength, which help build a foundation of strength and endurance for prewriting skills. All my classes loved it! To my surprise, a pediatric occupational therapist who taught a continuing education class that I took a year later highlighted that very same task. Ego now in check.

Finding Inspiration

This book was created from my binders of lesson plan notes, as well as presentations from my community speaking engagements. The goal was to create something easy and accessible for you to use in your preschool job or family life so you don't have to spend the hours that I did looking for ideas, scrolling through Pinterest, or reading complicated textbooks about the *why*. Our focus here is the *how*.

When I started, I couldn't find a single website or book that met all my lesson-planning needs. After a year or so of teaching, I found the book *Dance, Turn, Hop, Learn!* by Connie Bergstein Dow (2006). Dow's lessons highlight ways to incorporate movement with a simple format. They contain helpful suggestions for music and materials, with topics like "a secret map" or "cars." Another resource for me was Rae Pica, a renowned early childhood educator and a prolific author in the field of early movement education. Her books are a great primary resource, especially if you want to go deeper into the foundations of early movement education. Her resource books include specific curriculum activities.

Pica says that research confirms a correlation between physical activity and an increase in self-esteem, self-confidence, independence, and feeling effective. Research also finds that physical activity correlates with moral reasoning skills and even with popularity, she infers (Pica 2003). I don't think I can make that claim, but I can say that my students have enjoyed themselves, even if some were reticent in the beginning. It's OK for shy children to observe first. We learn in so many ways, through touching, looking, listening, and even smelling. In fact, I have had students who didn't initially participate in the activities of a movement class become my biggest and most active fans of the class by the end of the year.

My hope is that children who have experienced a movement program and activities like the ones in this book will develop a healthy lifestyle and find some type of movement activity they enjoy. A Zen proverb says, "Move and the way will open." This applies to young and old, but it's easier if we can develop this habit in our youth.

Teacher Education Requirements

Let's briefly look at educational requirements for preschool teachers. In general, preschool teacher requirements are not standardized across the United States. Requirements for public preschool teachers vary by state and employer. Preschool teachers in public school settings must (1) complete an approved teacher preparation program, (2) pass a state or national competency exam, and (3) earn a license or certification (Study.com 2017). Requirements for preschool teachers in the private sector also vary by state and employer.

The National Association for the Education of Young Children (NAEYC) lists six core standards for the education of early education professionals (NAEYC 2009). I recommend that you review this list at www.naeyc.org.

Currently, candidates for early childhood teaching positions may either be licensed or have earned a certificate from an accredited educational program. Programs granting associate's, bachelor's, and graduate degrees in early childhood education are accredited by the NAEYC, the National Accreditation Commission for Early Care and Education Programs, and the National Early Childhood Program Accreditation. Accreditation programs ensure that degree-granting programs meet specific standards. NAEYC supports the acceptance of an entry-level two-year associate's degree program because these programs offer opportunities to enhance demographic diversity of teachers.

What are the requirements for a preschool physical education (PE) or movement teacher? Although there are national and state standards for teaching PE to children in grades K–12, I am not aware of educational requirements for teaching PE or movement to preschool students.

Despite the lack of requirements for a preschool movement teacher, do not underestimate the benefit of a trained teacher. I agree completely with the National Institute for Early Education Research (NIEER), which says, "The better the teacher, the better the opportunities for the student" (NIEER 2017a). NIEER's *State of Preschool 2016* reports that thirty-five of fifty-nine state-funded pre-K programs require a "teacher degree" for preschool teachers, with nineteen of fifty-nine requiring an assistant teacher to have a degree. From 2013 to 2016, the number of programs requiring preschool teachers to have specialized training in early childhood education rose from forty-five to fifty-one. Although these gains are good, NIEER says that children in some states are still being left behind due to fluctuating quality standards (NIEER 2017b).

A government-funded program and resource that supports early movement education is Head Start, a program of the US Department of Health and Human Services (www.acf.hhs.gov). It provides comprehensive early childhood education, health, nutrition, and parent-involvement services to children and their families from lower-income backgrounds.

Why Add Movement Activities?

Developmentally focused movement activities help children form active habits, discover their bodies, learn self-control, improve self-esteem, increase independence, and build self-confidence. Research also suggests that birth to five years old is a critical period of development. The environment we provide children at this stage can influence their development.

These are your talking points if you are a preschool administrator or teacher justifying adding a preschool movement teacher position. Providing optimal opportunities to maximize growth and development for children is what parents and caregivers want.

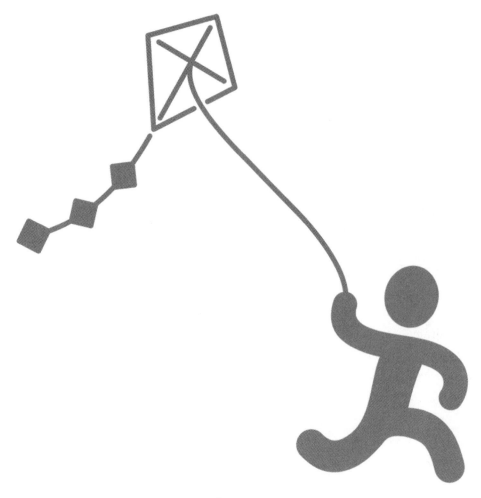

CHAPTER 2
Why Preschoolers Need Movement

In my movement classes, activities are geared toward children three to five years old. In general, children age two and younger do best in classes that include their parent or caregiver. They excel with the kind of one-on-one assistance that is possible with a ratio of one teacher to no more than ten students. Two-year-olds tend to play solo next to other children and are still learning how to play games in groups.

Learning and growth during the preschool years occur mostly through movement experiences or motor discovery. This is how preschoolers learn about themselves and their environment. Movement is the process and product of learning, according to educator Maida Riggs (1980).

Preschool means "before school." A movement curriculum during preschool prepares the child for elementary school. A mother from my drop-in movement class said that her son was initially nervous about starting school. He completed my weekly class with a confidence boost, excited to start kindergarten.

Exercise Is Not a Bad Word

Our bodies naturally want to move. We are designed for movement. It is society and our environment that limit or enhance our ability to move. Forming a positive attitude toward active movement early in a child's life sets the stage for openness to physical activity.

I have heard countless hospital patients moan, "Oh no, go away!" after I knock on their doors and say I am a physical therapist. If I use the word *exercise* in the same sentence, they usually grimace as they try to find an excuse to get rid of me.

The last thing I want is for a child to cringe when they hear the word *exercise*. I want children to grow older with an appreciation for movement and healthy activity. I don't want them to experience being the last student picked for a team in gym class or to doubt their abilities. Some of you may be thinking, "What a Pollyanna! Life is about letdowns." Yes, you are correct. I'm sure all of us have experienced this. Competition is inevitable, but why encourage it during the critical first five years of life?

If we have a secure foundation in learning movement strategies during our early years, these early experiences will overflow into other areas like language acquisition and social-emotional development. The ability to learn without the fear of losing and making errors supports confidence and a growing awareness of integrating and managing our body's movement.

Competing with Technology

Technology is a big roadblock to maintaining healthy attitudes toward movement. It's here to stay and designed to be addictive. A software designer who was interviewed on ABC's *20/20* said that games are created to stimulate dopamine responses in the brain (Vargas 2017). Those responses promote addiction. Plus, posture is greatly affected by gaming, with the norm being upper spine hunched forward, shoulders rounded forward, and head gazing down at the device. Not to mention that we are usually seated when using our phones or gaming devices. It's not just a phenomenon among older children; younger children are just as affected.

We want to take away all negative experiences for our children, but for most of us that's not possible. What we *can* do is build their motor self-esteem and resilience and increase their positive perception of exercise.

Nature versus Nurture

Scientists studying developmental kinesiology have debated whether genes (nature) are more crucial than experiences (nurture). Physical therapists believe that both our genes and our experiences matter, and PTs rely on Esther Thelen's dynamic systems theory. Basically, Thelen (1995) says that there are bodily subsystems that interact while a motor ability forms, without one subsystem being more important than another. All a therapist does is act on different subsystems to achieve a functional outcome or goal. This is what you want to do in your class: create an enriching environment to offer experiences that help build motor abilities.

Forming Habits

I've noticed an increase in research and books written about habits in adult self-development. *New York Times* best seller *The Power of Habit: Why We Do What We Do in Life and Business* (Duhigg 2014) talks about the science of the habit loop and what we can do to change bad habits. S. J. Scott's *Habit Stacking: 127 Small Changes to Improve Your Health, Wealth, and Happiness* (2017) encourages us to make small changes, to group the changes into a routine, and to use a trigger to remember to use the routine. The current thinking in the self-development field is that developing good habits is better than relying on willpower. It's not about forcing yourself to do something you don't want to do but, instead, establishing healthy routines.

Although these books are written for adults, the benefit of infusing healthy movement habits of any kind into a child's lifestyle early in life encourages exercise to become second nature and not a chore. Habits can be passed on in families. Some parents and caregivers don't like to lie on the floor to play. Some adults have disabilities that restrict their ability to move or get down on the floor. The infants in these families may spend more time in car seats and bounce seats, so they're less likely to lie on their stomachs. This may create tighter hip flexor muscles, less trunk extension, and decreased lower-trunk strength. No judgments. But wouldn't it be great to pause and provide opportunities for experiences that could enhance a child's development? We live in a dynamic system; why not add some dynamics?

Recess Is Not Physical Education

Here's one more thought for you. Some schools may say we don't need movement classes because we have playground time, but recess is not physical education. Recess is time that children can run, jump, and climb on outdoor equipment or run around in an indoor gym. Outside they can walk over uneven sand, grass, and mulch to challenge their balance. They can stimulate their nervous systems by rocking on the swings. Yet not all children are adventurous; some play in the sandbox the whole time, while some are intimidated by the line of children waiting for the slide. Children self-select play activities, and their playmates also influence their choices. I argue that play and a structured physical education class are both important aspects of social, cognitive, and physical development.

Children who are guided and supported by a teacher or parent to perform specific motor skills will have improved self-esteem, independence, and confidence. As adults, we take for granted that we can do certain tasks.

I remember getting frustrated with my son because he couldn't tie his shoes as we were heading out the door, already late for school. Then I realized that I had taught his older sister that skill easily because I could give her one-on-one attention. I had more time to teach her. My son had three sisters along for the ride, plus a stressed mom trying to get to school in a timely manner. I realized that I never really showed him *how* to tie his shoes, nor gave him enough time to practice and process the task. This happens in families that have the best intentions, mine included.

Discovery with Five Practices

I use the concept of guided discovery as defined by Riggs (1980). It breaks down the learning process into five steps of guided discovery: exploration, discovery, selection, repetition, and imitation. I translate these steps in the classroom in the following ways:

1 **Exploration**: Free playtime with scarves, balloons, or other objects.

2 **Discovery**: Using sports reporter language, describe what you see the child doing. "I see Philip spinning the scarf in a circle." "I see some children tapping their balloons into the air above their heads."

3 **Selection**: Ask the children to try to manipulate an object or a skill in a different way. "Can you try to balance the paper plate on your head?" "Can you move your balloon without using your arms and feet?" "Try, and see what happens."

4 **Repetition**: Stack skills in the same lesson. For example, do warm-up activities lying on the belly, then progress from lying on the belly to rolling on a mat, to crawling under an obstacle while lying on the belly. Weekly repetition is another strategy and involves incorporating skill sets learned previously into subsequent movement lessons.

5 **Imitation**: See-and-follow-me games support guided discovery. Examples include copycat and musical call-and-repeat songs, in which the teacher sings a verse with a movement, then the group repeats the verse and motion at the same tempo.

The most common mistake I see is too much instruction. Overteaching can minimize a child's self-confidence in skill acquisition. Allowing some room to make errors and explore self-correction is foundational to the learning process. Not every activity needs verbal and hand-over-hand instruction to do it the "right way." Allow some space for self-discovery. Find your balance by using the five practices of guided discovery.

CHAPTER 3
Motor Milestones

To think about growth, we look at motor milestones, defined as age-specific targets or achievements in the motor system. Please keep in mind a quote from Rae Pica (2003, 106) while reviewing the following motor milestones: "Motor development is age-related . . . not age-dependent." These milestones are only guidelines, best used as general goals. They are not intended to be used alone to assess a child's development.

Motor skills are classified into two types: fine motor and gross motor. I'll use the term *big-movement* for gross-motor skills. Fine-motor skills use smaller muscle groups like fingers and hands for precise, controlled movements. Big-movement skills include larger muscle groups and whole-body movements.

The following examples are the physical signs of progress toward mastering movement skills in a defined environment. They are listed according to the age ranges when they typically develop. Use these skill sets to determine which lesson plan is most appropriate for your group and which challenges could be introduced. Factor in your observations of the developmental stage of each child along with the general stage of the group as you approach each lesson plan. If you have a good grasp of typical development, you will be best prepared to create an environment that will increase the opportunities for success.

There are several online resources for motor milestones, with some minor discrepancies among sources. For this book, I referred to the following resources: the Centers for Disease Control and Prevention (www.cdc.gov) and LD OnLine (www.ldonline.org). Please note that these skills are not representative of every motor task but represent a snapshot of what to look for.

Two- to Three-Year-Olds

Big-Movement Milestones:

- runs forward
- jumps in place with two feet together
- stands on one foot with help
- walks on tiptoes
- kicks ball forward

Fine-Motor Milestones:

- snips with scissors
- strings four large beads
- holds crayon with thumb and fingers

Three- to Four-Year-Olds

Big-Movement Milestones:

- runs around obstacles
- walks on a line
- balances on one foot for five to ten seconds
- hops on one foot
- pushes, pulls, and steers toys
- rides tricycle
- uses slide independently

Fine-Motor Milestones:

- builds a tower of nine small blocks
- drives nails and pegs
- copies a circle shape
- manipulates clay material

Four- to Five-Year-Olds

Big-Movement Milestones:

- walks backward, toe to heel
- jumps forward ten times without falling
- walks up and down stairs independently, alternating feet
- bounces and catches a ball
- catches a thrown ball most of the time
- skips, alternating feet

Fine-Motor Milestones:

- pours
- cuts on a line continuously
- copies cross shapes and squares
- prints some capital letters

Five- to Six-Year-Olds

Big-Movement Milestones:

- runs lightly on toes
- walks on a balance beam
- hops
- skips, alternating feet
- can use a jump rope
- skates

Fine-Motor Milestones:

- cuts simple shapes
- copies a triangle and traces a diamond shape
- copies first name
- prints numbers one through five
- grasps a pencil
- has established handedness
- pastes and glues

You may observe a child ahead of or behind the milestones listed here. When that occurs, I often recommend the book *Growing an In-Sync Child* (Kranowitz and Newman 2010) to parents who have developmental concerns and questions. This book does a great job of summarizing children's motor development and growth. Parents worried about a child achieving motor milestones should always contact a medical provider for further assessment. I apply four foundational concepts from Kranowitz and Newman's book to my teaching philosophy:

1 Most children develop according to the same sequence but not at the same rate.

2 Childhood is a journey, not a race.

3 Slow is usually better than fast.

4 Having fun helps.

CHAPTER 4
The Structure of a Movement Class

Play is free-flowing and creative. You can have those elements in a movement lesson, but it is class structure that supports the complex and dynamic process of motor development.

Getting Started

Songs are a great way to start a movement class and to learn the students' names. They are also a fun way for a group of children to get to know one another at a party or meeting. An opening song helps set the pace of class and encourages participation. It provides structure by helping students anticipate that the group gathers in a circle for an introduction to one another and to the pending activity. Below are some sample opening songs; you can find more at www.atozkidsstuff.com:

- **"Good Morning"**: Sing, *"Good morning, (Keisha), good morning, (Keisha), good morning, (Keisha). Welcome to movement class!"* Move on to say the name of the next child. This song is good for younger children who may have reservations about participating.

- **"Hello"**: Sing and clap at the same time. Try a two-beat clap. First, clap hands against your lap (beats one and two), then clap hands together in air (one, two), then back to your lap and keep alternating as you sing:

    Hello, (Connor), hello (clap, clap) . . .

    (lap clap, lap clap) (clap hands, clap hands)

    (lap clap, lap clap) (clap hands, clap hands)

    Hello, (Susie), hello (clap, clap) . . . *Hello, (Amir), hello* (clap, clap) . . . *Hello, (Isabella), hello* (clap, clap) . . .

    Name all the children and the adult helpers, then end with, "Let's start movement" or "Let's get moving" or whatever phrase you choose.

- **"Where Is Thumbkin?"**: You can perform with or without the hand gestures. Teacher: *Where is (Name)? Where is (Name)?*

    Option 1: Child stands up and sings: *Here I am. Here I am.*

    Option 2: Child sits and points to self quietly while the group sings: *There is (Name). There is (Name).*

- **"Welcome Train"**: Sing the following to the tune of "A Hunting We Will Go."

    I'm glad I came to school, I'm glad I came to school,
    with all the other boys and girls, I'm glad I came to school.

    (Name) will be there. (Name) will be there,
    with all the other boys and girls, (Name) will be there.

Warm-Up Movements

Stories have a beginning, middle, and end, and so should movement classes. Schedules and patterns help form positive habits and behaviors. I like to start the preschool year with a similar beginning, and always use some type of closing activity at the end of each class to encourage successful transitions from the movement class to the next activity.

Start with a song. I use something I heard in my oldest daughter's preschool, *"Happy morning to you, happy morning to you; with bright smiling faces all over the places."* OK, so it's faulty English. But it has catchy lyrics and it lets the class know you are starting without having to say, "Eyes on me," "Waiting for quiet," or anything else that becomes annoying for the children and you.

Now, if appropriate for the lesson, show the equipment you will be using or discuss the theme. The key to success is to pick a theme you like. Otherwise it will not be fun (wink).

Exercise classes always used to start with stretching. However, now the recommendation from the American Academy of Orthopaedic Surgeons is to warm up muscles first with an aerobic activity like jumping jacks, walking, or big body movements (AAOS 2006). Then stretch after class to avoid injury.

Use a combination of fun, short follow-me songs and games to accomplish the warm-up. For example, most children really love the action song "Goin' on a Bear Hunt." I use pictures as visual cues, which a helper holds up while I use auditory and tactile cues to demonstrate the actions we need for the story. Then we sing and move as we act out the song. After moving to the Pacific Northwest, I realized the run-away-from-the-bear part of the song is not such a good idea.

That's why I now include a short talk after this activity about what we should do if we see a bear: slowly back up, make noise, and stay next to an adult.

Combine short, two-minute activities, one after another, for a child's version of circuit training, to enhance aerobic conditioning (refer to the sampler in appendix B warm-up). Try to keep in mind the area of the body you are focusing on, and choose warm-ups that mimic the movements or muscle groups you are about to use.

It seems like common sense, but I will say it anyway: choose warm-ups that are activity specific. If you have a throwing lesson, use warm-ups that focus on stretching arms up, out, and behind you. Trunk twists are also relevant in throwing overhand.

When my older children were involved in recreational sports coached by parent or student volunteers, it frustrated me that the coaches rarely encouraged consistent, appropriate warm-ups before playing the sport. This practice helps protect our bodies from injury.

Learning the Rules: Stop and Go Signs

For a successful lesson, children need to learn how to stop and go during a movement class. Many times you will have to halt an activity and move to another or stop because the children are getting too excited or bored.

This is my signature introductory activity, which can be reintroduced any time during the year with some alterations. In fact, I make a point to start the very first class with this activity and to use it again at various points throughout the year for reinforcement.

You don't have to spend money. I use cardboard signs cut in the shape of a red hexagon (Stop), a green circle (Go), and a yellow circle (Slow). My oldest daughter painted these signs years ago, and I still use them.

Ask the children if they pay attention to traffic signs when they're in the car with a caregiver or family member. "What do you do when you see this?" Pull out the Stop sign from a box or from behind your back. Of course, the children say, "Stop," because they are extremely smart, and you tell them so. Then pull out the green Go, ask what it says and "What do you do when you see this?"

Finally, tell them that you will trick them with your last sign. Show them the yellow sign and see if they can figure out what it says and means.

Take a few steps backward away from the line of children and explain that when they see the Go sign, they should walk toward you. Show them what that looks like. Then show them the Stop sign and ask them what should happen when they see that: stop. Finally, when the yellow Slow sign pops up, show them that their movements should be "like a turtle" or "like a snail" by moving very slowly.

Now have the children line up on a line of masking tape on the floor. Using a taped line helps them always know where to go back to, and you won't have to waste any time trying to line them up verbally.

Start by showing a sign and saying the action it specifies. Alternate signs slowly then quickly as the group gains skill at this activity. Then show the signs without saying, "Stop," "Go," or "Slow." You will see immediately which children rely on auditory commands.

The Body of the Lesson

These are the activities that focus on a lesson's theme or targeted motor skill. Activities can be set up with timed stations for the class to rotate through. Stations give the children a chance to try specific motor skills or to do an activity in a smaller group. The activities can relate to a theme or a motor milestone.

For example, let's look at the motor milestone of throwing. Between ages two and three, a child may be throwing in one direction. By age four to five, a child may be bouncing a ball and catching it most of the time. If you have a class of three-year-olds, bouncing and catching a tennis ball will not only frustrate many of them, but it may also frustrate you when the group loses interest in the task. This doesn't mean you can't start to practice a catching task. You just have to assess and present the skill on a continuum from easy to difficult. This will help those who haven't achieved the milestone while challenging those in the group who are ready for the next skill. Get the children to throw beanbags at a large target. (Beanbags will not roll away and cause mass chaos.) A large target encourages early successful experiences, which will build the foundation for more challenging throwing skills.

People lose interest so quickly that advertisers need to change the screen focus every couple of seconds to keep our attention. (Are you still reading, or have I lost you?) Likewise, it's best to keep the class moving by having children spend between seven and twelve minutes on each task. This will help keep their interest. In our age of information overload, our attention spans are shrinking.

Tip for a fun transition: Let them know it's time to stop an activity by sounding a sliding whistle.

Structured Yet Flexible Activities

Always go into your class with a plan; after class has started, modify the plan as needed. It's also wise to keep a back-up activity ready in case your lesson plan must be altered. This can be as simple as having a list of movement songs to play or using the Stop-Go-Slow sign game.

I want to expand on a couple of activities in a typical lesson plan so that you understand the process behind the selections. The first example involves activity stations: you take a group, divide the children into two or three smaller groups, and practice a skill set. I consistently find that small-group activity stations promote positive outcomes.

Throwing Stations

Station 1: Throwing Beanbags into Laundry Baskets

For a visual cue, show a simple picture of someone performing an underhand throw. This demonstrates what the throw could look like. Every so often, offer hand-over-hand instruction (with permission) to children if it seems they will be receptive or if they ask for this type of help. You can also step in if a child is showing signs of disinterest or stress during the activity. I usually try not to interfere immediately with tactile or verbal cueing until the children have processed the task on their own.

This activity can be easily modified for fun at home on a rainy day. Get your children to help you fold socks, and then toss the socks from a distance into the laundry basket. (This might get them excited about helping with chores.)

Station 2: Target Practice

Use a picture of a softball pitcher throwing overhand as a visual cue. Do not skip a demonstration of the task. Some children may be itching to do the activity, but others will need to watch you break down the task to enhance their learning. Especially with younger preschoolers, it's important to experience throwing with whichever hand or manner (underhand or overhand) feels comfortable to them. I rarely correct the mechanics of their throw during the exploration and discovery phases.

Add simple verbal cues to the demonstration: "Hand to ear, step, throw." While the children are practicing their throwing, you can repeatedly recite these auditory cues. Remember, we all learn in different ways: listening (ears), tactile (fingers), visual (eyes), and even olfactory (nose). So offer all of these experiences to your class.

Station 3: Teddy Bear Knockdown

This is totally the most fun station ever, in all the classes I have ever taught. Set up tables or a surface to the average height of the children's chests or slightly lower. Then line up teddy bears or other stuffed animals on the table. Use taped lines on the floor so the children know exactly where to stand. Marking lines is worth the extra set-up time before class because lines help minimize, and sometimes even eliminate, the number of times you'll have to say, "No, don't stand there," during class. All you must do is point to the tape to remind the children where to stand safely. Best of all, it empowers the children to be independent in their positioning during an activity. (Painter's tape is an essential supply.)

If you don't have enough teddy bears to knock down, another option is empty plastic water bottles. Fill them halfway with beads or beans and seal the cap with duct tape. When they are knocked down, they make a satisfyingly loud noise. Plastic bowling pins also make good targets to knock off the table. Use what you can find.

Music Lesson Example

Let's see how a music-focused movement class can be used to teach rhythm and tempo.

You don't need a music degree for this. All I had was a year of guitar lessons in elementary school and attendance at many choir, flute, and piano recitals of my own children. If you don't have that, do you have a radio? Then you can do this.

Of course, if you want to go beyond the basics, you could invite a talented professional music teacher to your preschool program or incorporate into your child's experience.

The body of this music-based lesson plan includes three activities that flow nicely into each other. You can always extend the amount of time in any activity if the children are having so much fun that they don't want to move on. It all depends on your time frame and the group.

Paper Plate Game

Here is a great way for children to learn names of body parts. Give everyone a paper plate. Then ask the class to "tap your head, tap your elbow, tap your toes, tap your nose" with their paper plates. The sky is the limit with this activity.

I love to try to rhyme the body parts and to include silly stuff like "tap your bottom" and proceed to giggle. Once the group has mastered this activity, try tapping slowly or rapidly. Perhaps even end with, "Now balance the plate on your head," or say, "Try to stand up," while the children are sitting. "See what happens!" You can add, "Now, balance the plate on your head while standing." Then do a huge fake sneeze while the plate falls off your head to the floor, and watch the class erupt in laughter or mimic your exaggerated sneeze.

Sticks

You may have heard of the task in which children hold a stick in each hand and hit the sticks together to copy a teacher's rhythms.

I fear mentioning the word *hit* and *sticks* in the same sentence, because I foresee a future incident report saying that a child knocked out a classmate. So instead, start with the children seated in a circle.

Stand up and say, "Watch me first." Demonstrate a slow tempo by beating a toy hand drum in a slow beat while walking slowly around the circle. The children will watch you intently.

Then stop drumming and walking. Ask, "What should we do when the drumming stops?" The children reply, "Stop." Then beat the drum quickly and walk faster around the circle. You can beat the drum even faster and run around the circle while saying that when the beat goes faster, you go faster, and you *stop* when the drum stops.

Before beginning this activity, try to make sure that all the children are listening with their ears or watching with their eyes. Then let the fun begin.

Free Dancing

Explain that it's now time for *free play*. This is time for self-movement exploration. Hand out ribbons, one per child, and explain that the children will start exploring and dancing with the ribbons throughout the allowed space while music is playing. Ask them what they think they should do when the music stops. Someone inevitably calls out, "Freeze" or "Stop." Then start the music and free play begins.

This stop-and-go task builds the habit of control, to divert internal attention to a task back to the teacher and group. This skill is necessary for group transitions, safety, and getting accustomed to being in a school-based setting.

Observe the group during free dancing. Offer one-on-one support if appropriate. It's also a great time to describe aloud the movements you see the children doing. For example, "I see Joe spinning in circles with the ribbon." This cueing indirectly gets other students excited about trying the movement.

It also reinforces and strengthens the self-esteem of the child performing the activity. It works: sooner than you know it, some children will be trying to think of new ways to use their ribbons. If creativity seems stagnant, say, "Everyone, watch this: Can you crawl with the ribbon?" "Can you put the ribbon in your other hand?" Or "Can you skip with the ribbon?" You get the idea, and so will they.

Winding-Down Activities

Every good beginning deserves a good ending. When you are having fun, it can be hard to stop what you are doing. Children, especially, can get upset with transitions. Establishing a consistent closure activity early during the movement class year is helpful. It can be as simple as stopping the last activity, gathering in a circle, and summarizing what the group just did in class, followed by singing a goodbye song.

> *Goodbye friends, goodbye friends,*
>
> *We'll see you soon again.*
>
> *Hope you had a happy day, happy day, happy day*
>
> *Hope you had a happy day. We'll see you soon again.*

Perhaps you're not fond of songs. Have the children "Stretch up high (speak in a high pitch), stretch down low (use a low pitch), stretch to the sides, stretch to your toes, stretch to your nose."

Maybe you want to teach them a Brain Gym maneuver (see pages 124–25), like the "Hook-Up" (Dennison and Dennison 2010). The Hook-Up uses the arms and legs to make a crisscross pattern, like making a pretzel with your arms and legs. Younger children can start by learning the first few motions of the pose; you can add a step at each class meeting until they master the full pose. Other age groups may be able to perform it immediately. Try not to underestimate your group. Look for effort, not perfection.

Choose a closure activity and stick with it for a while. Once it becomes anticipated, alter it to correlate with a new lesson theme, or add sign language to your goodbye song. Repetition initially helps create the structure of your class. Subsequently adding novelty encourages creativity and learning for all ages.

PART II
Let's Get Moving!

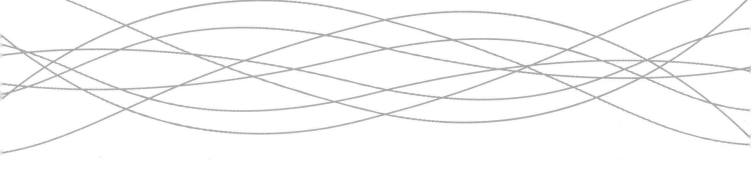

Enough foundation; the rest of this book is a series of lesson plans divided into topics for easier access. What follows are thirty-six complete lesson plans constructed from the perspective of a preschool movement class. However, many of these activities can be easily incorporated into a home-based child care setting, used at a child's birthday party, or added to a pre-school curriculum.

All you need to do is flip to a lesson page. Collect your supplies. Prepare and modify your environment. And have fun!

CHAPTER 5
Your First Movement Classes

These are your very first classes. It's a time to set expectations. Your children need to know where within your space they can safely go and what types of experiences they will have in movement class. It's time to get to know your students and for them to get to know you. Time to start remembering their names and observing the skill sets of the group.

This is also a time to build the class's interest in your activities. We do that by starting with the basics. For a baseball-themed lesson plan, say, "Baseball is a game you play with two teams." "A player will hit a ball with a bat." "This is what a baseball looks and feels like." Have the group pass the ball around the circle to feel and examine the ball.

Remember, not all children watch baseball at home. Some of them may not have the slightest clue what baseball is, while others may be on a Little League team already. This is an opportunity to get all the children on the same playing field since not every child has the same experience with baseball. (Yep, pun intended.)

Explain what a bat looks like. Then explain what a baseball field looks like: "The players play on a field shaped like a diamond." Hold up three shapes, one at a time: a circle, a diamond, and a square. Ask the group to clap when you hold up the diamond shape. Explain that each base is on a part of the diamond. Say, "Each baseball player takes a turn hitting the ball with a bat. As soon as a player's bat makes contact with the ball, the player drops the bat, runs to first base, then to second and third base, and then back to where they hit the ball." It's best to introduce only the running aspect first. Each child can pretend to swing and hit a ball. Then, as each child runs around the bases, the rest of the class is encouraged to say the name of each base out loud: "First, second, third." (This introduces math concepts.)

Lesson 1 *Our First Movement Class*

This lesson begins with body awareness. This is the ability to know where your body is in your environment. It's necessary for success in subsequent lessons with challenging motor tasks. Your warm-ups should be done one after another to keep your students engaged. The two activities help familiarize your group to directions and having fun.

If you have new students join your class, it's a good idea to revisit and repeat all or some elements of this lesson.

Supplies

- spots to sit on
- one plastic hoop
- Stop, Go, and Slow signs

Getting Started

Start with the group sitting in a circle on the floor. To show children where they can sit, I like to use squares cut from a yoga mat. Once all the children are sitting, start to wave and sing, *"Happy morning to you, happy morning to you; with bright smiling faces all over the places."* Learn the children's names: "Hello, (Name), hello." Repeat for each child. End with, "Let's start movement class!"

Place a hoop around you. Talk about your personal space and how people have personal bubbles. Then place the hoop around a child or another teacher; all eyes will be on you when you do this. Then proceed to sit inside the hoop next to the person already in it, not touching but a little too close. Inevitably, the other person inside the hoop will look very uncomfortable and the children will start to giggle. The aha moments start to happen as they begin to understand the concept of their own space and the "bubbles" around themselves.

Warm-Up

- Open and close hands while saying, "Open," "close."

- Point and flex feet while saying, "Point your toes. Flex your foot."

- Make corresponding arm and hand movements while you say, "Shake it out high, shake it low, shake it to the side, shake it behind you . . . shake it all about."

- "Ladybug, ladybug, touch your toes": Sit with legs straight out in front of you. Show pincer fingers. Jump the fingers down your legs starting at the upper thigh and ending at your toes. Then choose another creature, such as a butterfly. Say, "Butterfly, butterfly, butterfly," as you fly your fingers down your legs, ending with, "touch your toes." I love for the students to call out the name of an animal, and then we think of an action to use as we say the animal's name or make the animal's sound down to our toes. The children have a ton of fun, and they also get a gentle stretch in the back of their legs.

- Open and close your legs: Sit in a long sit (legs flat on the floor in front of you). Say, "Watch me and do what I do." Spread legs to form a V, then close them. Repeat. Make it fun by varying the speed at which you do this action. Try speeding it up so fast that it becomes too hard for the children to follow. This usually results in giggles.

- Peanut butter and jelly sandwich: Sit in a V sit. (This flows nicely from the previous activity.) Tell the class that you are hungry and you're going to make a PB&J sandwich. Ask leading questions, such as, "What do we need?" Pretend to grab the ingredients and tools from behind you. Ask the class to mimic you. Use the "table" space between your open legs to prepare the sandwich. The best part is to make your actions a little silly. When it's time to cut the sandwich, make big, diagonal cutting motions so the children will get a great inner leg stretch. You could even say, "Let's squash it, squash it, squash it." End with, "Let's *eat it*!" And proceed to gobble the sandwich with gusto.

- Bigger, bigger, jump: This needs no instruction. Just do it, and the children will follow naturally. Start in a squat. Say, "We are getting bigger and bigger, and jump!" as you slowly rise from a squat to a stand. End with a large jump. Repeat this activity a couple of times. (Squatting promotes healthy hips and knees. Please practice this on your own, but don't force it if your body has limitations.)

ACTIVITY • On Your Spot

Use seat markers or yoga squares to mark spots for the children to sit on in a circle on the floor.

Ask the children to stand on their spots. Then sit down and say, "Sit on your spot." Proceed to go through as many actions as you can think of, and use the milestones on pages 12–13 as a guide:

- Stand on your spot.
- Go next to your spot.
- Stand behind your spot.
- Stand on tiptoe on your spot.
- Stand on one leg on your spot.

- Walk around your spot.
- Stand in front of your spot.
- Jump on your spot.
- Sit on your spot.

ACTIVITY • Red Stop, Green Go, Yellow Slow

Ask the students to stand in a straight line along a line of masking tape on the floor. This activity works best with a larger space, but everything can be modified. You need three homemade or store-bought signs: a red Stop sign, a green Go sign, and a yellow Slow sign. Stand in front of the children and show them the signs one by one. Explain what each one says and what you do when you see that sign.

"When you see red, stop." "When you see yellow, move as slowly as a turtle." "When you see green, walk or run forward toward me across the room."

Be sure to hold the signs in a way that lets you switch them as the children move toward you.

Want to have fun? Wear a police officer hat and white gloves to pretend to be a crossing guard during the game.

Winding Down

Gather your group, either on the starting line taped on the floor from the previous game or in a circle on mat squares. Sing a goodbye song:

Goodbye, friends, goodbye, friends; we'll see you soon again;

Hope you had a happy day, happy day; hope you had a happy day;

We'll see you soon again.

> ### *Challenge*
>
> Once you have tried saying the action and showing it, show a sign as a visual cue without the auditory cue of calling out its action. Remind the children to *look* for what they are supposed to do and to pay careful attention. Make it more challenging by flipping through the signs at a faster pace.

Lesson 2 *Our Bodies, Our Space*

Lesson 1 intoduced body space. Now in lesson 2 you'll reinforce and develop these concepts further.

Supplies

- Hoberman sphere
- paper plates
- scarves
- five or six large hoops
- music (a Bob Marley reggae song works well with the "Island Hopping" activity)

Getting Started

Sing the song "Where Is Thumbkin?" You can do this with or without hand gestures.

> **Teacher**: *"Where is (Name)? Where is (Name)?"*
>
> **Option 1**: Child stands up and says, *"Here I am. Here I am."*
>
> **Option 2**: Child sits and points to self quietly while the group says, *"There is (Name). There is (Name)."*

Warm-Up

I was first introduced to a Hoberman sphere at a presentation by Kofi Dennis, master teaching artist with the Wolf Trap Institute for Early Learning Through the Arts in Vienna, Virginia. The sphere is an expanding and contracting ball, technically a spherical polyhedron, and is a great tool for showing expansion and contraction of a space.

"We will be learning about our bodies and the space around us." Show the sphere closed, then slowly open it while saying, "S-t-r-e-t-c-h." Slowly close it as you say, "S-h-r-i-n-k."

Hold it over your head and show the bubble of space around your own body. The children will love it even more if they get to go inside the sphere.

If you have a big enough model, you can fit a child's head and torso inside it. I've seen a specialty jumbo sphere that accommodates an entire child. If you place the sphere over one child as a demonstration, all will want to try it! I avoid this by demonstrating using only myself. Alternatively, have everyone hold a piece of the diamond-shaped corners of the sphere with one hand in a pincer grip. Then on a count of "One, two, three," have everyone gently pull out to open the sphere, then push in to close it. Say "pull" or "push." This can also be used as a group closure task for any lesson or as a classroom transition. You can then choose all or some of the following movements:

- Stretch and shrink, using arms and legs.

- Point and flex feet from a long-sit position.

- Ladybug, ladybug, get your toes.

- Open and close legs while long-sitting.

- Sit with knees bent in front; lift one foot up while straightening knee. Put foot down; alternate feet.

- Blow up pretend balloons. Sit with knees bent, feet flat on the floor in front of you.

- Lie on your belly. Be flying birds, lifting arms and legs off the ground for a few seconds. Repeat.

- Grow bigger, bigger, and jump.

ACTIVITY • Paper Plate Game

This is one of my favorites. It's best to have the children sit on place markers arranged in a circle on the floor. Use place markers that are the same color to avoid arguments starting with, "No, I want the yellow one!" Pass out one paper plate per child and ask the students, "Can you?" as you demonstrate how to use the plate with different body parts:

- tap your knee
- tap your toes
- tap your elbow
- tap your head
- tap behind your back
- tap your belly
- tap your bottom (be silly, if you choose)
- tap your thumb

ACTIVITY • Free Dance with Scarves

Choose a movement song. Technology makes this simple: look up a song online, download it, and play it, all in a matter of seconds. Use music that lasts an average of four to eight minutes to keep the activities and the students' interest in them moving along. **Tip**: Instruct the children before the activity starts so they understand your expectations.

Sit in a circle. Say, "Here is a scarf, one for each of you. Please sit and wait until everyone gets a scarf. When you hear the music, you can dance or move with the scarf any way you like." Remind the children to be careful of their friends and to stay in their own bubble of space.

"What should we do when the music stops? That's right: stop. Freeze." Use the freeze game with groups that attempt to run around with the scarves, especially if it appears that bumps and accidents could occur due to poor spatial awareness. Environmental management strategies work better than hollering, "No, stop! Don't do that."

ACTIVITY • Island Hopping

This is a noncompetitive version of musical chairs. It only takes a minute for you to set up the space while the children wait. Place hoops on the floor. Ask the children if they know what an island is. Talk about it being a piece of land surrounded by water. Show them a hoop and explain that each hoop is an island in the sea.

"When the music starts, you can fly around the islands by flapping your wings." Demonstrate by moving arms slowly up and down. "Whenever the music is on, you fly over the water. When the music stops, it's time to land on an island to rest."

The rules are that there is no limit to the number of people who can land on any island. All are welcome, even if they are only able to put a foot on the island. Then proceed to start and stop the music as the children follow your lead.

Winding Down

Using the song "The Hokey Pokey" provides an opportunity for the children to practice several things. They will practice naming body parts as they sing the well-known lyrics, and they will practice performing an activity in a group.

Challenge

After each time you stop the music, remove one hoop. The students will start to realize there are fewer and fewer islands to rest on when the music stops, so they will need to share an island so their friends can rest as well. For older children, you can play the game until there are only one or two islands left. This forces them to think creatively about how to share an island.

CHAPTER 6
Mix It Up: Integrative Lesson Plans

Integrative lessons combine different movement skills and concepts and involve many muscle groups. They require processing skills and multiple steps to complete. Keep in mind the needs of your group before you apply these lessons. Some groups need more exposure to basic motor milestone skills first, while other groups do well when starting with these integrative topics. Use lesson 3 to introduce the idea of moving in different ways. Use lesson 4's obstacle course to observe the skill sets your group has and which skill sets they need to develop.

Lesson 3 *The Quality of Movement*

This lesson works as a good introductory integrative lesson. I like to use this lesson in the middle of the school year as a reprieve from working on specific motor skills. It's also helpful to use this lesson when the class needs to enhance its ability to pay attention.

Supplies

- words on paper
- dark bag containing movement objects

Getting Started

Sit in a circle on mats to discuss the word *movement*. You could say something like "How does something move? *Movement* means 'in motion.' Things can move slowly or rapidly. Things can move with lightness or heaviness. What do you think?"

Warm-Up

- Walk around the circle to a song.
- Point and flex feet in a long sit.
- Open and close legs in a long sit.
- Make a pretend peanut butter and jelly sandwich.
- Be a seed and grow into a flower, stretching petals to the sun.
- Kick. Alternating legs, kick right, kick left, kick to the side, kick to the other side. Be sure to provide enough space between children's sitting spots.
- Squat down, then grow bigger, bigger, and jump.

ACTIVITY • Movement Words

Write words on construction paper. Show and say each word to the group, then try to perform that word. Get creative and use words like *jiggle, collapse, swing, melt, dart, stretch, flop, stomp, twirl, sneak, bounce, slink, crouch, soar, trudge, kick.*

ACTIVITY • Motor Skills

Use as much space as possible in the area you have available. Teacher and children move in different ways around the perimeter of the space or in a circle outside the children's sitting spots.

Walk like you are collapsing.

Waddle like a duck.

On tiptoe, stretch as high as you can.

Sneak. (If you want to add some theatrics, wear a bandanna over your mouth.)

March like a soldier.

Stomp like a dinosaur.

Run like you are moving through a room of water.

Run lightly and quietly.

Crawl.

You get the idea; make up movement ideas of your own.

ACTIVITY • Bag of Objects

Take a large, dark bag and fill it with a variety of items that have movement potential. Pull out one item at a time with as many theatrics as you can muster. Ask the children to try to move like the item. Ask questions like "What is this?" "How does it move?" and "Can you move like it?"

Here are suggested items and their associated movements:

- feather (float down to lie on the floor)
- spinning top (sit and spin, around and around)
- large exercise rubber band (hold with both hands and pull hands apart slowly; release hands quickly)
- bouncing ball (jump)
- spinning drum (stand with feet planted and swing arms from side to side)
- a toy with wheels (roll)

Winding Down

Keep it simple and end with a goodbye song (for example, see "Winding Down" in lesson 1 on page 28). These activities can take time.

Lesson 4 *Obstacle Course*

Use the following obstacle course lesson plan to observe the skill sets your group has and which skill sets it needs to develop.

Supplies

- sitting spots
- painter's tape or balance beam
- play tunnels
- hoops
- mat for rolling
- bubble wrap

Getting Started

Say, "Hello, (Name)," and clap. Sing and clap at the same time. Try a two-beat clap. First, clap hands on your lap (one, two), then clap hands together in the air (one, two), then back to your lap. Continue alternating clapping your lap and your hands as you sing:

> *Hello, (Connor), hello* (clap, clap) . . .
>
> (lap clap, lap clap) (clap hands, clap hands),
>
> (lap clap, lap clap) (clap hands, clap hands)

Or you can sing the rhythm like this, without lap claps:

> *Hello, (Susie), hello* (clap, clap) . . .
>
> *Hello, (Amir), hello* (clap, clap) . . .
>
> *Hello, (Isabella), hello* (clap, clap) . . .

Name all the children and adult helpers, ending with, "Let's start movement," "Let's get moving," or whatever phrase you want.

Warm-Up

Repeat most of the warm-ups from a previous lesson. Repetition is good for motor learning and provides security for children who may be slow to participate:

- Tap or rub arms and legs to "wake up." Say, "Wake up, arm," and, "Wake up, leg."
- Point and flex feet with legs out in front.
- Open and close legs.
- Count down to toes: "One, two, three, four, five." Or "Ladybug, ladybug, touch your toes."
- Sit with knees bent in front, and lift one leg up while straightening that knee; alternate legs.
- Blow up pretend balloons.
- Lie on your belly and hiss like a snake.

ACTIVITY • Obstacle Course

Set up a series of obstacles. Make the starting place obvious with a flag or sign. Tell the children, "Watch me first," while you show them what to do at each obstacle:

- **Balance beam**: Walk heel to toe along a line of tape on the floor.
- **Play tunnels**: Crawl through. (Place a mat under tunnels to protect little knees.)
- **Hoops**: Hop in and out of hoops (taped to the floor so they don't move).
- **Snake crawl**: Crawl under a long scarf tied between two chairs or cones.
- **Roll on mat**: Assist students one-on-one. Ask the child to lie down like a snake. Log roll along the length of the mat, with arms at sides if possible. Carefully guide the student as needed for safety. Notice that this skill set precursor was also in the warm-up.
- **Sensory station**: Tape bubble wrap or foam on the floor for the children to walk on, hop on, or stomp over.
- **Repeat obstacle course multiple times**. If time allows, turn the group around to reverse the order.

Winding Down

Sing a goodbye song (for example, see "Winding Down" in lesson 1 on page 28).

Lesson 5 *Yoga Time*

You don't have to be a yoga expert for this lesson. If you have limitations, such as a bad knee or sprained wrist, you can still model poses. Explain how bodies are all different, and show how you'll modify the pose yourself. "Just try, and see what happens," I say.

Supplies

- yoga mats (optional)
- pictures of yoga poses

Getting Started

Start in a circle with students sitting on spots on the floor. One year I had a class in which I needed to assign spots to separate friends who became a little too distracted when sitting next to each other. But, in general, I like to allow students a choice of where to sit.

Ask the class, "What do you think we are doing today?" Write the word *yoga* on a large paper easel. Ask if the students can guess what the word is. It is likely one child will say, "Yoga." Proceed to give a simple explanation of yoga:

- Yoga means unity.
- It started thousands of years ago in India.
- It teaches us to breathe and to use our minds and bodies together. It's about strength and flexibility. (Using silly bicep gestures and stretching motions helps explain.)
- Yoga movements are called *poses*, and they sometimes look like animals.

Warm-Up

Assess the overall energy level of your group. If the class has high energy, start immediately with the breathing techniques. If the class is more reserved with low energy, get up and walk around the perimeter of your space first. Observe your students' needs.

ACTIVITY • Warm-Up: Just Breathe

- **Bunny breathe**: Inhale three times quickly through the nose, followed by one long exhale out the nose.

- **Peace breathe**: Breathe in through the mouth, then breathe out through the mouth while saying, "P-e-a-c-e."

- **Balloon breathe**: Raise arms while inhaling (which expands ribs to allow more air in), then lower arms while exhaling. Fun twist: make this final breath a silly balloon breath. Inhale very big, then exhale and twist and wither to the floor like a balloon that has been let go. Have fun demonstrating this motion by using a real balloon.

- **Take-5 breathe**: Count, "One, two, three, four, five," while you breathe in, then count, "One, two, three, four, five," while you breathe out. Try saying it out loud first, then do it without words, using your hand to count five seconds on your fingers.

ACTIVITY CHOICE • Summer or Autumn Yoga Story

Yoga mats come in child sizes. Having multiple mats is useful, but if finances don't allow you to buy them, there are alternatives. You can buy mildly sticky foam cabinet liners on sale. They last for about two years of occasional use before losing their grip. They're easy to cut to the perfect preschool size and cheaper than buying adult-size yoga mats. You can also use blankets on top of a rug.

Autumn Yoga Story

A large flip poster board or easel with pictures of each pose is a good supplement for your physical demonstration. If the students do not understand your verbal explanations or demonstrations, they can look at pictures of the poses, which are inspired by www.kidsyogastories.com:

- Days are getting shorter (crescent moon pose).

- Tree leaves change color (tree pose).

- Birds fly south looking for warmer weather (warrior 3 pose).

- Farmers harvest their crops on their tractors (chair pose).

- Whales migrate south along the coast (whale pose).

- Foxes grow thicker fur. Look up at the moon and yip like a fox (tall kneeling pose).

- Monarch butterflies fly south to their winter home (butterfly pose, also known as cobbler's pose).
- Hedgehogs hibernate (child's pose).

Additional poses are described below in "Quick and Simple Yoga Poses."

Spring-Summer Yoga Story

You can make up any yoga story using the following story about a sunny day as a guide. The boldfaced words indicate when you can strike a pose that resembles a word in the story.

The **sun** wakes you up. (Stretch arms and legs out wide or perform the good morning sun pose, described in "Quick and Simple Yoga Poses" below.)

You look out a window and see a big evergreen **tree**. (Tree pose: balance, standing with one foot on top of the other.)

You see a **butterfly** that has landed on a tree branch. (Butterfly pose: sit with bottom of feet together and move knees up and down.)

You slowly gaze into the distance and see a **tall mountain**. (Mountain pose: stand tall, head up and arms at your sides.)

Something strange is in the sky. Could it be a **bird**? (Warrior 3 pose: flap your arms like a bird or extend arms out to the sides and lift one leg in the air behind you.)

You **stretch from side to side** to see. What is it? Could it be? (Do side trunk stretches with arms raised, gently leaning to each side.)

It's a green and purple **dragon**! (Dragon breath pose: kneel with torso straight up, stick out tongue, and exhale forcefully out your mouth.)

Quick and Simple Yoga Poses

- **Good morning sun pose**: Reach up to the sky, bend down to touch the toes.

- **Tree pose**: Balance on one foot if possible, then balance on the other foot. Modify for younger children so that they extend their arms up or out to their sides, with one foot resting on top of the other.

- **Butterfly pose (cobbler's pose)**: Sit with bottoms of feet together and flap knees up and down gently as if they are wings.

- **Downward-facing dog pose**: Place hands and feet on the floor, with bottom up toward the ceiling and head down. Your body forms a V.

- **Snake pose**: Lie on belly, push chest up off the floor with arms, and hiss.

- **Bow pose**: Talk about a boat on a lake, saying that the front of the boat is its bow. Lie on your belly, bend knees, and lift feet off the floor while reaching back with hands to grab your ankles or feet.
- **Mountain pose**: Stand tall.
- **Triangle pose**: Stand with legs open and arms outstretched. Reach down with one hand to touch the opposite foot (modified version).
- **Dragon breath pose**: Sit in a tall sitting position or on bent knees, simulate a baby dragon breath, and then simulate a big daddy breath with tongue out.
- **Final pose options**:
  - **Child pose**: Curl up with knees bent, chest on knees, and forehead on the floor with arms resting at sides.
  - **Resting pose**: Dim the room lighting. Lie on back with arms and legs outstretched and relaxed.
  - **Legs-up-the-wall pose**: Sit as close as possible to a wall, swing legs and feet up, and rest them on the wall. Lie on your back. Dim lights.

Challenge

Place a beanbag on each child's belly while they are in resting pose. You can choose to instruct the students to have their legs resting flat on the floor or lifted with feet on a wall. Ask your students to take belly breaths so they move the beanbag up and down. "Move the beanbag without your hands; use only your belly."

Add a tactile option during resting pose. Place a beanbag, rubber ducky, or small stuffed animal on each child's belly without any verbal instruction. I like the weight of a beanbag as it provides good feedback to the primary breathing muscle, the diaphragm.

Add an auditory option. Play soothing music for a few minutes during resting pose.

Add an olfactory option. Place a few drops of lemon or peppermint essential oil on a tissue, and during resting pose, waft the smell over the children's noses, preferably with their eyes closed. Ask them to think about what they smell. When they open their eyes, you can talk about what they think it smelled like.

Winding Down

Quietly whisper a goodbye song (for example, see "Winding Down" in lesson 1 on page 28). Use repetition by singing a familiar song or add novelty by singing it in a quiet voice (which is rare for me).

Optional closure: "In some yoga classes, the teacher may end with the word *namaste* and bow the head forward. Namaste means the peace within me greets the peace within you." Show the children how to place their hands together and bow with their heads coming forward.

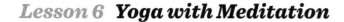

Lesson 6 *Yoga with Meditation*

I like to use this lesson when teachers tell me that the class needs calming activities. I remember having a blast with a class whose energy level was high. But I sent the children back to their classroom very excited. Oops. The teacher had difficulty getting them to calm down for his next quiet activity. This lesson is the remedy for that.

Supplies

- mats for children (be creative)
- projector, screen, or TV to play a video
- blankets (optional for resting pose)
- essential oil and napkin
- quiet instrument or singing bowl (an inverted bell that produces a vibrating sound when its rim is stroked with a mallet)

Getting Started

Begin this lesson sitting in a circle. Ask, "Do you know what yoga is?" Allow each child to offer a brief explanation. "Let's spell *yoga* together: *Y, O, G, A*." Then proceed to explain and demonstrate the warm-up.

Warm-Up

Hands-on-the-wall game: Children line up and walk along a wall, touching cutout handprints taped low and high (but within reach) along the wall. Do this activity if time allows; otherwise, begin this lesson with a yoga video.

ACTIVITY • Yoga Video

The children will become super attentive when you add a video to a lesson plan if it's not something you usually do. It never ceases to surprise me how this focuses the class. I do this only once per school year to keep it a novelty.

Consider picking different video clips from the suggested DVDs below, or use your own favorite. Choose parts of the videos based on how much time you have.

- *Once upon a Mat*: Nine easy-to-learn yoga adventures (Namaste Kid 2012)
- *Storyland Yoga* (Playful Planet 2010)
- *YogaKids: Silly to Calm* (Wenig 2004)

Here's a sample eleven-minute yoga sequence from *Once upon a Mat*:

1   Wake up (four minutes)
2   In the garden (three minutes)
3   Tropics trail (four minutes)

ACTIVITY • Meditation for Kids

Set up the environment as you transition the children off the video. Dim lights if possible. Lower your voice so that the class must quiet down to hear you.

- **Beginner mantra**: "Sometimes in yoga, people may say a phrase again and again. Let's try: 'Peace begins with me.' Say it as many or as few times as you feel works."
- **Breath work**: Breathe in for four short breaths; breathe out in one long breath. Try this a few times.

- **Legs-up-the-wall pose**: If you have the space, have the children place their bottoms next to the wall with their legs resting straight up against the wall. Ask them to close their eyes. This is a beneficial position for the immune and circulatory systems.

- **Resting pose with olfactory stimuli**: While the class is resting, tell the children you will walk by them with a smell. They can inhale deeply with their noses, but ask them not to say out loud what they think the smell is. "Keep the idea in your mind." Use an essential oil, like lemon, on a napkin and wave it in front of their noses as you walk by each child.

- **Resting pose with auditory stimuli**: It's time to use your singing bowl or to play an instrument. If you don't have access to these items, you can rub the rim of a glass cup of water to make a gentle sound. Have the children close their eyes while you make the sound. Talk about the sound after a few minutes of resting pose. Most groups usually last about three minutes in this pose before at least one child wants to start talking or begins squirming. But don't let that stop you from trying this. I am always surprised by how many children enjoy even one minute of silence. After this experience, some children will ask me if we can spend more time in resting pose next time.

Winding Down

Take a few minutes to talk about the olfactory or auditory experience the class just had. Let the children take turns guessing what the scent or sound could be. Explain that some yoga teachers may end their session with the word *namaste* and a bow of the head forward to each other to show respect and thanks. *Namaste* means "the peace in me greets the peace within you." It's simple, and I feel it does not promote any agenda, thus allowing you to respect all cultures represented in your classroom (this list is for your convenience, but we recommend you confirm pronunciation and accuracy).

You can share ways to say "peace" in different languages: *salam* (Arabic); *héping* (Chinese); *kapayapaan* (Tagalog); *paix* (French); *frieden* (German); *eirini* (Greek); *shaanti* (Hindi); *pace* (Italian); *heiwa* (Japanese); *pyeonghwa* (Korean); *mir* (Russian); and *paz* (Spanish).

Challenge

With children sitting cross-legged on the floor, ask them to place the pinky finger and thumb of one hand together and to do the same thing with the other hand. Then, maintaining fingers of both hands in the same position, instruct the children to rest both hands on their knees, with palms up, while they sit.

Lesson 7 *Balloons*

Playing with balloons is 100 percent joy. This lesson may appear to be fun, but your hidden agenda teaches science concepts, body awareness, and teamwork.

Supplies

*   bulk balloons (use the same color to prevent children from becoming upset at not having a certain color)

Getting Started

*   **Don't say a word.** I'm usually very verbal with the children in my class, so this gets their attention immediately. Take a balloon, blow it up with bravado, and let it go flying around the room.
*   **You are the balloon.** "Can you fill yourselves up with air?" "Blow, blow, blow, while your arms are getting bigger and wider." Then let out the air and fizzle to the floor.
*   **Helium balloons.** Helium is a gas that is lighter than air, and you can put it in a balloon so that it floats. "Has anyone seen a helium-filled balloon at a birthday party? Let's fill ourselves up with helium and float around the room. When I tap you on the head, can you pop and fall to the floor? Remember to stay there until *all* the balloons, all the children, are popped."

Warm-Up

Warm up large- and small-motor muscles.

*   Open and close your hands in front of your body.
*   Open and close your hands with arms out to the side.
*   Shrink and grow: Tuck knees into chest and place your head down on your knees, then open arms and legs wide.

ACTIVITY • Great Big Balloon

Everyone holds hands in a big circle. Ask the group to walk slowly into the middle of the circle until all are as close as is comfortable. "We are going to be a *big* balloon that we will fill up with our breath to make bigger. Blow, blow, blow."

As the group does this, begin to walk backward to expand the circle, while still holding hands. Once the circle is as big as possible, tell the children to gently let out the air and come forward to the middle of the circle and sit on the floor. Repeat until they master this action.

Challenge

Instead of holding hands, use a large piece of elastic. Fabric stores sell elastic bands about six feet long, which you can tie into a loop. Ask the children to stand in a circle, hold on to the elastic loop, and not let go. (Otherwise, someone could get a painful snap.) Ask the children to walk into the middle of the circle while still holding the elastic. Then ask them to walk backward slowly so that everyone can feel the stretch of the elastic in their hands.

Want to make it more challenging? Float around the room as a group, holding the elastic. Try to turn the group in a circle in one direction, then in the other direction, while all children continue holding the elastic band.

ACTIVITY • Free Play with Balloons

Big smiles always accompany this activity. Give each child a balloon. Turn on a song and let the children explore what they can do with their balloons: tapping, jumping, hitting, and twirling. Anything works song-wise, but my favorites are the corny ones like "Balloon Song" (Johnny 2003) or the classic "Chim Chim Cher-ee" (Van Dyke et al. 1997).

Allow for exploration. Be a sports announcer during free play. Comment on what you see as you walk around the group. "I see LaVonne tapping her balloon up high." "I see Amir balancing the balloon on his head."

If the children are less adventurous, encourage them to try different actions by asking, "Who can show me how to move the balloon across the floor without using your hands?" "Let's see what happens" is a great phrase to use to keep the group focused on expectations about the experience, not on the outcome.

Winding Down

- Do gentle stretches.
- Take-5 breathe: breathe in for a count of five; breathe out for a count of five.
- Sweep arms up to the sky and down to the toes.
- Circle arms out to the sides.
- Gently twist from side to side.
- Stand with feet flat on floor, rise onto tiptoes, repeat.

Lesson 8 *Creative Ways to Use Hoops*

This hoop lesson will develop large-motor skills. Use your age-appropriate milestones to choose movements to try. Two- and three-year-olds learn to jump in place with two feet together. Demonstrate how to hop in and out of the hoop with two feet. Your four-year-olds can stand in the hoop and hop on one foot. Five-year-olds can skip around the hoop (see pages 12–13 for milestones).

Supplies

- one toddler-size hoop per child
- beanbags
- music

Getting Started

Show the children the hoops. Talk about their shape, what they are made of, and what you can do with them. Then pick a classic icebreaker song, like "The Wheels on the Bus." My favorite version is by MaryLee Sunseri (2001c), a singer from Monterey, California. I have fond memories of her singing in her home-based preschool music class that my children and I attended.

Warm-Up

Walk, jog, or skip around a circle. Use cones or sitting spots arranged in a circle to encourage the shape. Add a challenge: demonstrate and ask your children to try to walk heel to toe around the circle.

ACTIVITY • Try It

Give each child a hoop. Ask, "What can you do with the hoop?" Allow for some free exploration. Then demonstrate different things you can do with a hoop:

- Swing it in your hand.
- Put your arm through it and rock it over your elbow.
- Walk through it.
- Twirl it around your waist.
- Place it on the floor and hop inside it.
- Place it on the floor and hop out of it.
- Place it on the floor and walk around it.
- Spin it on the ground.

ACTIVITY • Toss It In

Start with all hoops on the floor, a few feet in front of the children's sitting spots. Give each child a few beanbags. Ask the class to try to toss the bags, one at a time, into the middle of a hoop. Have free play (see below) if interest and time allow.

ACTIVITY • Free Play with Hoops

Time to turn on music and allow free play with hoops. Set a timer and remind the children that when the music stops, they should freeze and listen for instructions about the next game.

Winding Down

Place a few of the hoops on the floor and ask the children to sit in a circle around the hoops. Join hands. Stand up.

Sing "Ring around the Rosy" while walking around the circle. Walk and sing slowly at first, and then speed up the song and walking pace as the children are able. Remind the children to let go of their neighbors' hands before they gently fall to the floor. Otherwise, with some groups you will likely hear "Ouch!"

Ring around the rosy, pocket full of posies,

Ashes, ashes, we all fall down.

Lesson 9 *Rhythm and Music*

This lesson introduces the joy of music. After a tactile warm-up, you start with an action song. I enjoy classic action songs, but feel free to replace with your preference. This lesson has three activities. Paper Plate Beats challenges the children to find rhythm with a common object. The next activity engages the entire body in learning about varying rhythms. Finally, the repeat-after-me song stimulates memory.

Supplies

- two sturdy paper plates for each child
- one drum or two sticks

Getting Started

Explain what *rhythm* is. Rhythm is a regular, repeated pattern of sounds. Examples of rhythm instruments include drums, sticks, rattling eggs, and tambourines. If you have any of these items, do a show-and-tell. Beat is the rhythmic movement or speed of music (Mullett 2013).

Warm-Up

Ask your group to gently tap or rub up and down their arms and say, "Wake up, arms!" then gently rub or tap up and down their legs and say, "Wake up, legs!"

Action song: "The Wheels on the Bus."

> When the wheels in the song are going around and around, make each hand into a fist and twirl your forearms around each other.

> When the wipers on the bus are swishing, swish the palms of your hands back and forth.

> When the horn on the bus is beeping put the palm of your hand in the air and make a pushing gesture.

> When the doors on the bus are opening and shutting, make a door with your hands and open and shut them.

> When the driver on the bus says, "Move on back," point backward over your shoulder.

> When the babies on the bus say, "Wah, wah, wah," turn and twist your fists next to your face.

> When the parents on the bus say, "Shush, shush, shush," hold a finger to your mouth and say, "Shhh."

> Repeat the first verse and say the last line slowly: "All through the town," to finish.

ACTIVITY • Paper Plate Beats

Sit in a circle. Each child gets two paper plates. Demonstrate the following actions, and ask the group to try to do what you do.

- Tap plates together.
- Swish: rub backs of plates together in a circular motion.
- Practice simple beats. You do it, then the group tries to imitate you. Slowly build complexity with the rhythms.

Here is an example of creating tapping and swishing sounds with the paper plates. You go first, then your students copy what they hear and see.

> **Teacher**: Tap, tap
>
> **Students**: Tap, tap
>
> **Teacher**: Tap, swish, swish, tap, tap
>
> **Students**: Tap, swish, swish, tap, tap
>
> **Teacher**: Swish, swish, tap
>
> **Students**: Swish, swish, tap

ACTIVITY • Drumming around the Circle

Children sit in a circle on their spots. Show what you expect. "I am going to play my drum and move around this circle." Tap a drumbeat at a walking pace while you walk around the circle. Ask, "What should I do when the beat stops?" "Yes, I stop."

Tap a beat at a slower pace while walking very slowly around the circle. Tap a beat at a faster pace and either run or walk quickly, depending on your space and children's dispositions. Personally, I love to run if it's safe to do so in the space available. Then ask the group to walk according to your drumbeat. (This is a crowd-pleaser.)

ACTIVITY • There Was a Great Big Moose

The origin of this American oral tradition camping/scout song is unknown, but it is fun to sing for all ages. It's a repeat-after-me song. The teacher sings first. The rest of the group will mimic what you say and do. Make antlers with your hand on top of your head when you sing "moose." Drink a pretend glass of juice by making a cup with your hand and placing it to your lips. Lie down when the moose goes to bed in the song. Touch your hair when the song says "hair." End the last verse with a full-body wiggle with hands sliding back and forth along your sides to show that the moose is sticky all over.

> You sing: *There was a great big moose!* Class sings: *There was a great big moose!*
>
> You: *He liked to drink a lot of juice.* Class: *He liked to drink a lot of juice.*
>
> You: *Singin' oh way oh.* Class: *Singin' oh way oh.* You: *Way oh way oh way oh way oh.* Class: *Way oh way oh way oh way oh.*
>
> You: *The moose's name was Fred.* Class: *The moose's name was Fred.* You: *He liked to drink his juice in bed.* Class: *He liked to drink his juice in bed.*
>
> You: *Singin' oh way oh.* Class: *Singin' oh way oh.* You: *Way oh way oh way oh way oh.* Class: *Way oh way oh way oh way oh.*
>
> You: *He drank his juice with care, but he spilled some in his hair.* Class: *He drank his juice with care, but he spilled some in his hair.*
>
> You: *Singin' oh way oh.* Class: *Singin' oh way oh.* You: *Way oh way oh way oh way oh.* Class: *Way oh way oh way oh way oh.*

You: *Now he's a sticky moose.* Class: *Now he's a sticky moose.* You: *Because he's all covered in juice!* Class: *Because he's all covered in juice!*

You: *Singin' oh way oh.* Class: *Singin' oh way oh.* You: *Way oh way oh way oh way oh.* Class: *Way oh way oh way oh way oh.*

Winding Down

Sing the goodbye song (for example, see "Winding Down" in lesson 1 on page 28) or tap a rhythm to repeat.

Lesson 10 *Movement Songs*

This lesson offers music and song activities with large-motor movements. It introduces an activity that requires playing with a partner.

Supplies

• painter's tape

Getting Started

Sit in a circle and sing a classic preschool song. Try "The Itsy-Bitsy Spider" or "The Wheels on the Bus," both with hand motions, or "Shake My Sillies Out" (Raffi 1996). Use a song you like or base your song selection on a learning theme. You can also choose a song you think the group will connect with the most.

Warm-Up: Clap and Follow

Children sit in a circle. Clap your hands on your lap in a pattern. "Clap, clap." Ask the children to listen to your rhythm and try to repeat it. Make the patterns more difficult with each repetition.

Don't forget to have some fun. Maybe end with a superfast clap or some silly under-the-knees claps. Get a good laugh going.

ACTIVITY • Row, Row, Row Your Boat

This is an old song whose lyrics I learned as a child. Use tape to mark two parallel lines on the floor, or arrange sitting spots on the floor so that each child will sit facing a partner. Each partner's feet face the other's, with knees slightly bent or straight. The straighter the legs, the better the hamstring muscle stretch. The various heights of the partner groups may dictate if the knees are bent or not.

Ask the children to reach forward across their legs to their partners and gently hold hands for the song. Demonstrate first.

Sing "Row, Row, Row Your Boat" while holding hands with a partner and rocking back and forth to the tempo of the song. I find that it is easier to modify the tempo as needed if you sing this song rather than if you use a recorded version of it.

Start singing and rocking slowly, then try a moderate pace. Finally, challenge the children by singing at a very fast pace or by adding a funny verse.

> *Row, row, row your boat*
> *Gently down the stream.*
> *Merrily, merrily, merrily, merrily,*
> *Life is but a dream.*
> (Repeat)
>
> *Row, row, row your boat*
> *Gently down the stream.*
> *And if you see a crocodile,*
> *Don't forget to scream. Aghhh!*
> (BusSongs.com, accessed 2017)

Winding Down

Sing a goodbye song (for example, see "Winding Down" in lesson 1 on page 28).

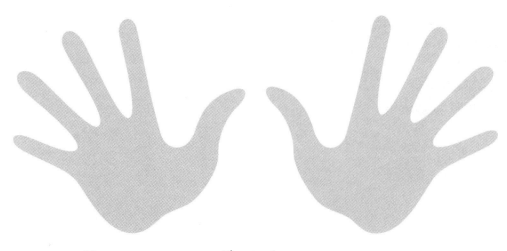

Lesson 11 *Movement and the Macaw Story*

Everyone enjoys a fun movement story. Use this story or be inspired to create your own.

Supplies

- two long scarves per child
- large picture of a tree

Getting Started

Share pictures of the specific animals in the warm-up: bunny, bird, snake, monkey, and mouse. Ask the children to help you identify each animal. Then start the warm-up.

Warm-Up

Play the song "Animal Rap" on *Preschool Action Songs 1* (Soloway 2013). Children sit in a circle on their spots. This action song directs their actions and movements. All you need to do is model the actions and call out reminders during the song:

- Hop like a bunny.
- Fly like a bird.
- Slither like a snake.
- Move like a monkey.
- Scamper like a mouse.

ACTIVITY • The Macaw Story

- **Time**: five minutes for the story and five minutes for free flying.
- **Music ideas**: "Dragonfly Hang" (Gara 2009) or "Red Rhythm Dragon" (Asher 2002).
- **Story**: use any motion you desire wherever you see a boldfaced word in the story.

Once upon a time, there were (state the number of children in your class) beautiful, colorful **macaws**. Did you know that the scarlet macaw is the national bird of Honduras? Anyway, the macaws all lived happily in a very large **tree** in the rain forest until one day people with large axes came and chopped down the tree to use it for firewood. **Chop. Chop. Chop.** The tree fell **down** with a loud crash.

The macaws were so **scared** that they all flew off in different directions.

There was still hope, as the macaws were generally **happy** birds and knew they could find each other as well as a new home. So they **flapped their wings** and flew through the jungle, following the drum sounds of the forest until they found their new home.

Now, give each child two long scarves and ask the class to fly around the space while the music plays, flapping the scarves as if they were bird wings. Encourage the children to flap their arms the whole time without pause. This is a wonderful shoulder-strengthening and endurance activity.

When the music stops, the children should stop flying and find their new home. Once I was lucky to have access to a four-foot-tall plastic tree that I moved into the center of our space. The students could place their scarves onto the plastic tree leaves to make their "nests." You can also draw a tree on a large piece of paper and tape the picture to a wall. Show the children that they can gather around the tree and build their new home in it by placing their scarves on the tree. If you use a paper tree, place the scarves at the base of the picture to build a group nest.

ACTIVITY • Free Play with Hoops

Choose a song that inspires you. Allow children to experiment with their hoops for a few minutes. This is free-play exploration time. Be sure to tell the group ahead of time what your stop signal will be so they know exactly when free time is up.

Winding Down

Sing a goodbye song (for example, see "Winding Down" in lesson 1 on page 28).

CHAPTER 7
Developmental Milestone Lesson Plans

The next nine lessons focus on big-movement milestones of locomotion, balance, throwing, catching, and coordination. The hand and finger lesson develops fine-motor skills, practicing different activities for pincer grip coordination and strength.

Lesson 12 ***Basic Locomotor Skills***

Locomotion is how to get from one place to another. It's about walking, jumping, and skipping. You'll go on a pretend journey using various skills and reinforce various types of locomotion with demonstration and practice in "Locomotor Skills Lineup."

Supplies

- "Goin' on a Bear Hunt" song (Greg and Steve 2000)
- pictures of scenes
- painter's tape

Getting Started

"Goin' on a Bear Hunt" is a call-and-response song. Review the actions in the song with the children before the music starts. This will help the students keep up with the song and feel more successful.

Warm-Up

Say, "In this song, we will sing about a camera, and this is what we will do." Gesture with your hands as if you are taking a picture with a camera.

"We may go through a field. Can you say 'swish'? While you say 'swish,' slide your left and right hands back and forth across each other like you're washing your hands. Your hands are the tall grass that swishes as we walk through it."

The version of the song cited above has the following order of scenes to act out:

1 Click the camera.

2 Open the door.

3 Walk on the road.

4 Walk through the wheat field.

5 Cross the bridge.

6 Climb the tree.

7 See the river.

8 Row the boat.

9 Tiptoe into the cave.

A flip chart or slide show with basic pictures of each location is an effective visual cue. YouTube has a few options as well. A song like this is great as an aerobic warm-up, and children really love it. Just be sure to educate them afterward on what they really should do if they see a bear while hiking in the woods.

ACTIVITY • Locomotor Skills Lineup

Use a visual cue by taping painter's tape to the floor in a line. The children stand on it and face you. Then use an auditory cue by singing while you demonstrate:

Put your hands on the wall, on the wall.

Put your hands on the wall, on the wall.

Put your hands on the wall, and do not let it fall.

Put your hands on the wall, on the wall.

Observe motor milestones by making mental notes of each student's abilities as the group performs the following activities across the classroom space and back again. Engage all forms of learning in your instructions: visual, auditory, and tactile.

Visual: Say, "Watch me first," and then perform the task. This is always helpful for those children who need to see a movement before they do it. It's important to do this even if other children are chomping at the bit to get going. You will probably see a few false starts, but do this step anyway for your visual learners.

Auditory: Explain a movement as you perform it, but keep the explanation simple. For example, repeatedly say, "Sidestep, sidestep, sidestep."

Tactile: If a child doesn't seem to understand what is expected and is getting frustrated, try gentle, one-on-one tactile cueing, but always ask the child's permission first. You can say, "Is it OK for me to touch you on your arm to show you the movement?" Allow for some struggle, trial, and error before you offer tactile help.

Ask the children to do the following:

- Walk forward.

- Walk backward.

- Sidestep.

- March, bringing knees up high with each step.

- Crawl.

- Gallop, taking a big step forward, with one foot in front of the other.

- Skip. Step and hop, alternating feet.

- Tiptoe.

- Run. It's always fun to call this action out loud since it's OK to be a bit loud in movement class.

- Repeat any of the above or come up with your own ideas.

Winding Down

Gather students in a circle. Perform some cooldown activities that involve gentle stretching, followed by a goodbye song (for example, see "Winding Down" in lesson 1 on page 28).

Try these cooldown actions:

- Seated in a long sit, point toes and flex ankles.

- Count down to toes (hamstring stretch).

- Open and close legs.

- Make rainbows with legs open (stretch arms from side to side).

Lesson 13 *Locomotor Skill Stations*

Locomotor skills are the movements we use to get from one place to another. These skills include the action of the legs in walking, skipping, hopping, galloping, marching, and jumping. They also include actions of the arms or entire body. For example, locomotor skills employed by a child who uses a wheelchair could include using arm and trunk muscles to push the wheelchair in the desired direction. A seven-month-old baby uses both arm and leg movements to crawl. All of these activities integrate locomotor skills.

Supplies

- sitting spots
- lily pad pictures or pieces of a yoga mat (ideally, a green one)
- teddy bear
- cones or painter's tape to mark boundaries
- music

Getting Started

Go back to chapter 4 and choose a "Getting Started" activity (see sample opening songs on pages 14–15).

Warm-Up

Children stand in a circle on their spots and perform the following actions:

- Reach up to the sky.
- Touch toes.
- Sweep arms to right, left, high, and low.
- Make arm circles with arms out to the side.
- Open and close legs while standing (starter jumping jacks).
- Rotate the trunk. With feet planted in place, swing arms around to the front and back.
- Stretch the trunk to the side. Saying, "Tick tock goes the clock," and with arms out to the sides, move trunk and arms to right and left sides.

- Touch elbow to knee. Place a sticker on each child's right knee and left elbow. Instruct your students to tap that elbow to that knee. Then tap the nonstickered elbow to the nonstickered knee.

- Do a crab lift. Sitting with knees bent and palms on the floor behind you, lift bottom up off the floor into a bridge position.

ACTIVITY • Locomotor Stations

Set up three stations with one adult at each station. If you have two teachers for a class of fourteen students, use only two stations. Divide the children into equal groups for each station. You will be more successful if you have an adult or teacher at each station. If this isn't possible, you can always move the entire group from one station to the next. Your space and number of students will determine this. Use a timer to signal the end of allowed time at each station.

- **Lily pad hop**: Secure pictures of lily pads (or pieces of a yoga mat) to the floor. Children hop to each pad by jumping with two feet together. Be sure to try different arrangements of pads and make the distance between them manageable. Include at least one challenging hop that may be farther away from the other pads.

- **Teddy bear run**: This is a relay run. Instruct the children to line up. The first child takes the teddy bear and runs with it down to the end of the space and back before passing it to the next child. The focus of this activity is cooperation, so having only one group doing this at a time avoids parallel teams, which tend to encourage competition.

- **Crab walk**: I find that crab walking is getting harder and harder for the technology generation of children. They lack upper-body strength and endurance, which makes the crab walk an important activity to do. Intentionally use the crab pose in your warm-up lessons prior to this class. This is a challenge station, and I have had many groups complain, "This is too hard." Upper-body muscle endurance needs time to develop, so you can choose to spend less time at this station or do stationary crab lifts instead.

This lesson can be modified using different versions of stations: Kangaroo Jump, Beanbag Run, Balanced Heel-Toe Walking with colored masking tape on the floor, or Galloping with a Toy Horse. Incorporate whatever works for you or for the supplies you have on hand. Remember that assessing the group's strengths in the earlier lessons will help determine what will be useful for your modifications.

Challenge

Place a chair across from the line of children. Tell the first runner to run with the bear to the chair, leave it there, run back, and high-five the next runner, who will then run and retrieve the bear. This adds multiple steps and may confuse the adult helpers, but try it anyway. I promise you will have fun with it.

Winding Down

Play the song "Penguin Dance Chant" (Hartmann 2010). **Warning**: this song is seriously addictive. I love its moderate rhythm. Listening to the song and singing along gives you a break from being in the lead all the time. All you do is demonstrate the actions while the song lyrics lead your group.

Tip for younger children: Briefly practice the movements described in the song before you start the music. This song may evoke giggling.

Lesson 14 **All about Balance**

You may be surprised to learn that a motor milestone for three- to four-year-olds is to balance on one foot for five to ten seconds. A child who can accomplish this can also successfully climb up and down stairs with one foot on each step.

Your class will balance an object and balance their bodies for this lesson.

Supplies

- spots to sit on
- one beanbag for each child
- tape or some type of balance beam
- DIY wobble boards

Getting Started

Sing a good morning song. Sitting in the circle, instruct the group to "Stand up if you _____." Children stand up briefly if the sentence applies to them and then sit down. Here are some sample options:

- Stand up if you are wearing something red.
- Stand up if you have brown eyes.
- Stand up if you have blue eyes.
- Stand up if you are wearing sneakers.

- Stand up if you like apples.
- Stand up if you have a younger brother.
- Stand up if you have an older sister.

Warm-Up

Select a few warm-up activities from appendix B that you have tried out in other lessons. Your goal is to build different skill sets over time with continued practice.

ACTIVITY • Beanbag Balance

Give each child a beanbag. Demonstrate ways you can balance it on your body. "Can you balance it on your hand? Can you balance it on your head? Can you balance it on your back? Can you balance it on your foot?"

ACTIVITY • Balance Beam Obstacle Course

Create an obstacle course that is all about balancing. Use tape on the floor, a balance beam if available, pool noodles, or foam mats. Be creative.

ACTIVITY • Wobble Board Practice

A large selection of wobble boards are available for purchase, or you can make a version yourself. Take a piece of a pool noodle and place a piece of very sturdy multilayer cardboard across it. Help children, one at a time, step onto the cardboard, with one foot on either side of the noodle. Be sure to guard them with adult hands during this activity.

Winding Down

Sing a goodbye song (for example, see "Winding Down" in lesson 1 on page 28).

Lesson 15 *Kicking*

This lesson introduces how to kick a ball. You will notice the warm-up focus is on stretching and moving the legs. Watch and observe how the children perform the ball skills. Can they place one foot up on the ball? If this is difficult, revisit balance activities in subsequent lessons.

Supplies

- spots to sit on
- balloons for each child
- balls made of crumpled paper (one for each child)
- orange cones with flat tops (one for every two children)
- foam balls (if available)
- playground balls (one for every two children)

Getting Started

Children sit on their spots and sing a favorite class song together to start the lesson.

Warm-Up

- Point and flex feet.
- Walk fingers down the legs, count backward, and then jump fingers down to your toes.
- Open and close legs.
- Stretch up and to each side.
- Stand on one foot, then on the other.
- Hop on one foot.
- Kick forward, to the side, and backward.
- Do donkey kicks: with hands on the floor, kick one leg off the floor, then the other, as able.

ACTIVITY • Dribbling Skills

Explain and demonstrate a "little kick," gently tapping the ball with the instep of your foot so that the ball moves forward a few inches in front, alternating feet for your kicks. Proceed and say, "little kick, little kick" to move the crumpled-paper ball across the space. Then "little kick, little kick" the balloon across the space.

ACTIVITY • Small-Group Skills

Separate your group in half. It's best to have enough supplies for each group. For example, if you have a total of eight children with four in each group, use four cones to practice kicking skills at station 1. Use four playground balls to practice ball skills at station 2.

Station 1: Kicking skills. Place a foam ball or balloon on a small cone. Ask the children to kick it off, then replace it and try again.

Station 2: Ball skills. Each child gets a ball. Try the following actions:

- Place one foot on the ball.
- Place the other foot on the ball.
- Put your hand on the ball.
- Sit on the ball.
- Put the ball between your feet.
- Walk around the ball.
- Put the ball between your knees. Can you walk without dropping it?

Winding Down

Choose a few easy activities to stretch the legs or arms (see appendix B).

Lesson 16 *Bring on the Balls*

In this lesson, you start with show-and-tell of three different size balls. Do not underestimate the importance of this "Getting Started" activity. Then do a detailed warm-up followed by a unique activity that encourages posture, back strengthening, and respiratory endurance. The final activities introduce catching in a way that supports skill development with minimal frustration.

Supplies

- balls in three sizes (big, medium, small) and of different materials (such as foam or rubber)
- mats to sit on
- small, lightweight plastic balls
- painter's tape
- trainer tennis balls (one per child, with some larger and some smaller)
- playground rubber balls

Getting Started

Start by singing a quick good-morning song to get the children's attention (see examples on pages 14–15). Or, if they are already focused, omit the song and dive into a discussion about the three different-size balls you have.

"Which is the largest ball?" "Which ball is the smallest?" After discussing size and names, you could also talk about densities of balls. Foam balls can be squished easily but can't bounce well. Rubber balls can bounce when dropped on the floor. Choose two balls, hold them up, and ask which one will bounce higher when dropped. Take guesses first, then demonstrate. Try comparing different balls. This introduces science concepts.

Warm-Up

- Take-5 breathe.
- Raise arms up and breathe in. Bring arms down and breathe out.

- Sit cross-legged on the floor, make spider fingers, and crawl your spiders away from you and then back. Crawl spiders on a diagonal away from you and repeat a few times in different directions.

- With legs straight in front in a long sit, point and flex feet.

- If you are fluent in another language, try saying "open" and "close" in that language to add a little diversity.

  - *Abierto, cerca* (Spanish)

  - 開いた *aita*, 閉じる *tojiru* (Japanese)

  - *Ouvrir, fermer* (French)

  - *Öffnen, schließen* (German)

  - खोलना *kholana*, बंद करना *band karana* (Hindi)

- Sit with feet in front and knees bent. *Stomp.* Alternate loud and soft stomps. It's fun to make noise when you are often told to be quiet.

- Lift both feet up into a V sit. Hold briefly; replace feet on floor. This motion strengthens abdominal muscles.

- Do crab lifts. Sit with palms on the floor behind the body, knees bent with feet in front, and lift bottom.

- Form each hand into a pincer like a crab. This is a good warm-up for throwing skills.

- Grow bigger, bigger, and jump.

ACTIVITY • Ball Blow

The aim of this activity is to start to work the respiratory muscles as well as to increase time spent in spinal extension. Resting on the belly with the arms in front for support helps build endurance and improves low muscle tone.

Arrange mats in a small circle. I split my class into two groups with at least one adult in each to help maintain fair play. Have five or six small, lightweight plastic balls for each group, but start by giving only one ball to each group.

Everyone lies on their bellies with arms propped up on elbows. Do not use hands. Tell the children to use their mouth and breath to blow the ball to a friend across from them. Have a group of thinkers? Don't tell them anything. Ask them to problem-solve how to move the ball around and into the middle of the circle without using their hands.

Challenge

Add more balls to the middle of the circle.

Children with low muscle tone tend to have floppy posture, with the trunk flexed forward and a lack of visible strength. These children will not like being in this position at all and will try to sit up or roll out of the belly posture. They will need encouragement to maintain it.

It's important to start with one ball in each circle of children. Instruct them to blow the ball to a person across from them, who in turn blows it to another friend.

Be sure all the children get turns, or they will tell you about it. Remind them that if a ball goes outside the circle, an adult will retrieve it. You want to maximize their time in trunk extension on their bellies.

ACTIVITY • Bounce and Catch with Trainer Tennis Balls

Use two sizes of trainer or junior tennis balls of similar color. These balls are softer, bounce more slowly than regular tennis balls, and are perfect for children's learning. Using two sizes helps diversify skill levels by giving a larger ball to the children who need a larger target and a smaller ball to those who may be able to handle a challenge. Of course the children don't know this. They see only that they are getting similarly colored balls.

Use blue painter's tape to mark the line where you want the group to stand. Sometimes I put small, evenly spaced pieces of tape perpendicularly along the line to designate spots for each child to stand. This ensures space between each child. The less time you spend telling the children where to stand or go means more time playing and learning; preparation is key. Try not to underestimate how helpful preparation can be for the flow of your class.

Demonstrate how to hold the ball in front of your chest or belly. Then drop the ball and try to catch it as it bounces up. Trainer tennis balls have the perfect bounce height for a preschooler of average height.

Always remind the children before they start bouncing and catching, "It's fine if the ball rolls away. Just go get it and return to your spot."

ACTIVITY • Rolling the Ball

Challenge

Have a few regular tennis balls on hand for children who find the slower bounce of the trainer tennis balls too easy. Say, "Here, try this one. When you bounce the ball, does it feel the same as or different from the ball you were just using?" The children will be too busy focusing on their own ball or running after it as it rolls away to pay attention to who has which ball.

This is another crowd-pleaser. Use tape to mark two parallel lines on the floor three to five feet apart. Separate the group into pairs, with each child sitting on a line facing his or her partner. Explain the activity before you distribute balls or expect distractions.

Have the children sit in a V sit, legs open to create a space for catching the ball. Each child on only one side of the line will get one ball after the verbal instructions and demonstration.

Verbal cues to catcher: "Hands ready; fingers stretched wide."

Verbal cues to ball roller: "Look at your partner; make sure they are looking at you. Roll the ball slowly into the opening between their legs." Tell the class to call out their partner's name before rolling the ball to be sure the catcher is paying attention.

Monitor this activity while standing up to help collect stray balls and observe skills.

Winding Down

Collect balls. Sing a goodbye song (for example, see "Winding Down" in lesson 1 on page 28).

Lesson 17 *Throwing Skills*

Most children begin to throw a ball overhand by the age of two. Your goal is to provide fun opportunities to learn this skill.

Supplies

- painter's tape
- laundry basket or similar container
- folded or balled-up socks (provide at least five pairs per child)
- beanbags (provide at least five pairs per child)
- eight to ten teddy bears, stuffed animals, or plastic bottles
- target (a nylon picture of a bowling set or a cardboard box, with holes of different sizes cut in either the picture or the box)
- Wiffle balls (provide at least two times as many balls as there are children)
- medium-size exercise ball

Getting Started

Sing a good-morning song (see examples on pages 14–15).

Warm-Up

- Stand up.

- Take-5 breathe.

- Stretch arms up to the sky and down to the toes.

- Make arm circles. With arms stretched out to the sides, make small circles in the air.

- Twist, gently rotating arms to one side then the other.

- Do shoulder shrugs.

- Sitting with knees bent, stomp loudly, then softly; repeat a few times.

- Be a carousel. Sit with knees bent; turn around and around (works best on a smooth floor).

- Do crab lifts. Sit with knees bent, place palms on floor behind you, lift bottom up, hold for a few seconds, and repeat.

- Grow bigger, bigger, and jump.

ACTIVITY • Throwing Stations

Set up well-defined areas for stations. Divide your group evenly between the stations with one adult to monitor each station group. Use tape on the floor or signs to indicate where the children stand during each task. This helps maintain the flow of the class and keeps you from having to give constant verbal reminders. Demonstrate each activity first to engage the visual learners.

Keep verbal instructions simple. Having an adult to supervise each station is the key to success. (For more information on throwing stations, see chapter 4.)

- **Underhand throwing**: Provide a large basket of rolled socks. Instruct children to pick up and throw one sock at a time, underhand, into a laundry basket or similar container.

- **Teddy bear knockdown**: Line up teddy bears, stuffed animals, or empty plastic bottles on a surface that is not higher than the average preschooler. Mark a line on the floor a few feet away from the targets. Be sure to instruct the small group to throw all the beanbags from the line first; then, after all have been thrown, the children retrieve them and try again.
- **Overhand throwing**: For a target, I use a nylon picture of a bowling set, with holes slightly bigger than a Wiffle ball cut in the material. Hang it up to use as a target for throwing balls through the holes. Another option is to take a big box, cut a hole in it, and decorate the outside with any theme; the children will throw balls into the hole. Putting a rug or blanket under the target minimizes the risk of balls rolling away.

Winding Down

Use a medium-size exercise ball about three feet in diameter. This size is large enough for preschoolers to hold it overhead with their elbows straight and arms open wide.

Have the class stand in a line with feet facing forward. Give the ball to the first child in line and ask the children to keep their feet facing forward. Have the first child pass the ball over their head to the person behind them without dropping it.

The ball gets passed all the way to the back of the line and then back to the front of the line in the same manner. This will require the children to turn to face in the opposite direction while staying in the same line.

Now add trunk rotation. With feet facing forward, the children pass the ball along their left sides from the front of the line to the last child in line. When the ball reaches the end of the line, the children pass the ball forward along their right sides.

Try passing a smaller ball along the line under the legs. The goal is to build cooperation, coordination, trunk flexibility, and communication among the children.

Lesson 18 *Catching*

I don't recommend teaching throwing and catching to preschoolers in the same lesson. These are different and complex skills.

Three activities are presented to the children. You'll use the practice of discovery in "Scarves Up." "Roll the Ball" is the practice of selection. "Drop and Catch" highlights how to provide repetition to learn how to catch. Review "Discovery with Five Practices" on page 10.

Supplies

- sitting spots
- one scarf per child
- painter's tape
- all-purpose balls (one for every two children)
- trainer tennis balls (one for each child)

Getting Started

Ask the children to look at the lesson supplies. "What do you think we will do today?" Tell them they'll learn to catch a ball. Proceed to demonstrate the steps of how to catch by saying, "Watch me as I lift up this ball, let go, then open my hands, bring them together, and catch it."

If a child is successful, then challenge them to try to drop and catch with one hand. I like to intentionally demonstrate a missed catch and use it as an example of progress, not perfection.

Warm-Up

- Take-5 breathe.
- Sit cross-legged on the floor. Walk spider fingers out in front and back, and out to the sides and back.
- In a long sit, point and flex feet.
- Open and close legs.
- Do trunk rolls. Sit with knees bent, feet together in front, and place your hands on the floor behind you for support. Then gently drop both knees to the floor on one side, then to the floor on the other side.

- Blow up pretend balloons. Sit with knees bent and feet in front. Pretend to blow up a balloon until it gets so big that you roll gently onto your back.
- Grow bigger, bigger, and jump.
- Draw figure eights in the air with hands clasped together and fingers intertwined.

ACTIVITY • Scarves Up

Each child gets a scarf. Demonstrate first, then ask the class to try it. "Try to throw the scarf up in the air and catch it before it touches the floor."

Scarves are a good way to introduce catching. There is a little more material to grab than with a ball, and they fall slightly slower than a ball.

ACTIVITY • Roll the Ball

Learning to catch is easier if you take legs out of the picture first. Pair up your class so children sit across from each other. Sitting prevents children from wandering and encourages them to focus on their partners.

A line of painter's tape on the floor is very useful for directing children to sit across from a partner without wasting time moving them into position. After the children are seated, hand out balls to all children in one row.

Verbal cues to catcher: "Hands ready, fingers ready and stretched wide."

Verbal cues to roller: "Look at your friend, say their name, and gently roll the ball toward them."

ACTIVITY • Drop and Catch

Give each child a large-size trainer tennis ball. These have a delayed bounce, which allows increased processing time for catching. The bounce height is perfect for preschoolers.

Verbal cues: "Drop the ball at chest height. Catch with two hands coming together."

Winding Down

Sing a quick goodbye song (for example, see "Winding Down" in lesson 1 on page 28). These activities will take time, so use a brief closure.

Lesson 19 *Coordination with Knock-Knock Balloons*

This is about having fun! Coordination is a complex skill, so focus on the practices of imitation and discovery for this lesson.

Supplies

- one knock-knock balloon per child
- one jump rope per child (those without plastic handles are safer; I prefer cotton ropes with a knot at each end)

Getting Started

Punch balloons are balloons you can find at party supply stores; they have a large rubber band attached to one end. You grab the band in your fist and punch the balloon back and forth. I realized quickly that it might not be the best idea to say the word *punch* with a group of young children, which is why I use the term *knock-knock balloons*. (Thank you, Fort Hunt Preschool threes teacher Rose, who coined this term.)

Sing and perform an action song. Choose a song below or one you like:

- "Head, Shoulders, Knees, and Toes"—try MaryLee Sunseri's English and Spanish version called "Head and Shoulders" (Sunseri 2001a)
- "Clap Your Hands" (They Might Be Giants 2005)
- "Shake My Sillies Out" (Raffi 1996)

Warm-Up

Focus on coordination skills:

- In a long sit, point and flex feet.
- With arms out to the side, touch one finger to your nose and bring it back out to the side; do both sides.
- Sing the "Itsy Bitsy Spider" using pincer grip fingers.

- Touch fingertips together, then push fingers in and out.

- Sit with knees bent and bottoms of feet touching each other.

- Get on the floor on hands and knees; pretend to be a cat, and say, "Meow." Try lifting one arm up. Try lifting one leg up. Ask, "What happens?"

- Place knees and hands on floor; keep knees on the floor and walk hands forward away from you. This is a starter plank pose.

ACTIVITY • Free Play with Knock-Knock Balloons

Demonstrate how to use these balloons. Give each child a balloon. Start together.

Verbal cues: "Like you are knocking on a door" and "Knock-knock with a fist."

ACTIVITY • Jump Rope

It's not easy to learn how to jump rope unless you learn the basics first. The expectation for preschoolers is to learn the sequence of movements, not necessarily to jump rope successfully.

Instruction: Show how to hold the rope. Place the rope behind your back while holding each end in the corresponding hand. Flip the rope over your head to the front, step over the rope, repeat. You may need to use hand-over-hand instruction.

Verbal cues: "Flip over head," "Step." Challenge: "Flip over head," "Jump." Try it faster. Keep in mind that those children who can't do the basic movements could get frustrated. Quietly adding a challenge for the appropriate children usually limits any frustration that could result from a group announcement.

Winding Down

Regroup. Choose a song to sing, or do one of the crossing midline activities found in "Exercise Your Brain" on pages 123–25.

Lesson 20: ***Let's Jump Rope***

This lesson is perfect for young preschoolers to begin to learn the component parts of how to jump rope minus frustration. Coordinating a jump rope is a milestone for five- to six-year-olds.

Supplies

None

Getting Started

Sing a good-morning song (see examples on pages 14–15).

Warm-Up

- In a long sit, point and flex feet.

- Open and close legs.

- Open legs. Count down to touch toes: "One, two, three, four, five."

- Close legs. Count down to touch toes: "One, two, three, four, five."

- Butterfly pose: Sit with bottoms of feet together and move knees up and down.

- Downward-facing dog stretch: On hands and knees, walk hands forward until belly touches the floor, then walk hands backward into downward-facing dog pose.

- Grow bigger, bigger, and jump.

ACTIVITY • Jump Rope

Here is one way you can determine the correct rope size for each child: Place the rope on the ground and have the child stand on the middle of the rope. Have them pull the handles up to their armpits. If the tips of the handles rest in their armpits or between the armpit and shoulder, the rope fits their size. If the handles go above the shoulders, it is too long and you should get a shorter one. A jump rope that has handles that don't come up to the armpits is too short (Revermann 2017).

Rope actions:

1   Stand up.

2   Extend arms out to the side at about forty-five degrees from the torso, with thumbs pointing out.

3   Jump on the balls of your feet.

Try:

1   **Shadow jumping**: Hold rope in only one hand and swing rope on one side of the body.

2   **Slow step**: Hold a rope end in each hand with the rope behind the body, use wrist action to flip rope forward over the head, step over rope, and repeat.

3   **Slow jump**: Hold a rope end in each hand with the rope behind the body, flip rope forward over the head, jump over rope, and repeat.

ACTIVITY • Group Jump

Have teachers or helpers hold a long jump rope along the floor. If you don't have a long jump rope, tie two handle-free jump ropes together to create one long rope.

Wiggle the rope gently on the floor. The children line up and take turns jumping over the wiggling rope.

ACTIVITY • Learn a Jump Rope Song

Song 1: "Teddy Bear"

Teddy bear, teddy bear, jump around (jump).

Teddy bear, teddy bear, touch the ground (squat and touch the ground).

Teddy bear, teddy bear, tie your shoe (bend one knee down and pretend to tie).

Teddy bear, teddy bear, read the news (pretend to hold newspaper).

Teddy bear, teddy bear, that will do (pretend to nap).

Song 2: "A Sailor Went to Sea"

A sailor went to sea, sea, sea (interlace fingers and make waves with arms).

To see what he could see, see, see (mime using binoculars or look through hands held in the shape of binoculars).

But all that he could see, see, see

Was the bottom of the deep blue sea, sea, sea.

Winding Down

Sing a goodbye song (for example, see "Winding Down" in lesson 1 on page 28).

Lesson 21 *Fingers and Hands*

Let's discover what we can do with fine-motor skills by using our hands to do activities that strengthen the hands and fingers. The following activities are a good precursor to writing skills.

Supplies

- one sheet of small stickers per child
- sheets of paper with hearts drawn on them
- clothespins in different colors
- boxes
- one quarter (or other coin)

Getting Started

Start with a brief group discussion about all the ways you can use your hands and fingers. Say, "Now let's move the fingers. Wiggle your fingers. Touch each finger to your thumb. Point your thumb up with your hand. Point your thumb down with your hand. Spread your arms out wide to the side and touch your finger to your nose. Touch your other arm's finger to your nose. Finish by hugging yourself."

Warm-Up

Choose warm-up activities from appendix B.

ACTIVITY • Hearts on the Wall

Give each child a sheet of small stickers. Before class, draw hearts on sheets of paper. Attach the papers to walls around the room at preschooler-head level. The children should stand by a paper that has a heart picture, peel off one sticker at a time, and place it on the outline of the heart. This allows them to repeatedly practice pincer grip. Plus, reaching up the wall is great for the shoulder muscles.

ACTIVITY • Clothespin Match-Up

Get boxes and designate each one a different color. Find clothespins that match the color of each box. Scatter the clothespins throughout the floor space of your room.

   The rules are to pick up only one clothespin at a time. Emphasize this to the children, as they will tend to grab as many as they can at one time. When a child picks up a clothespin, he needs to find the matching colored box, use pincer fingers to pinch open the clothespin; and attach the clothespin to the side of the box. Repeat until all clothespins have been matched to boxes.

ACTIVITY • Crossing Midline

Instruct the class to alternate touching one hand to the opposite side's knee. Say "touch" while you demonstrate.

ACTIVITY • Group Coin-Pass

Everyone stands in a circle with the palm of one hand facing up. Start the coin pass by placing a quarter in the palm of one of your hands. Take the hand with the quarter and pass it to the palm of the person next to you by flipping your hand over onto their hand. Repeat so that the quarter gets passed around the circle of hands.

Winding Down

Sing a goodbye song (for example, see "Winding Down" in lesson 1 on page 28). Add hand gestures or waving to your song to increase the complexity of a familiar activity.

CHAPTER 8
Sporty Lesson Plans

Preschool is a wonderful time to learn about all the activities we can do with our bodies. Some children have already mastered the motor skills needed to play a sport without frustration, yet many others must first develop their motor skills before being introduced to a sports league. Preschool is a good time to get children interested in various sports without the pressure of game day or parental expectations. The goal is to build confidence and self-esteem without pressuring the students to make the winning goal.

Lesson 22 *Learning about Athletics*

This lesson's focus is an introduction to sports: what a sport is and how different sports can be from one another. This lesson is about using matching and identification skills. It is also about learning how to coordinate effort with a friend, which introduces the idea of teamwork.

Supplies

- spots to sit on
- various sport pictures that are cut in half

Getting Started

Welcome and good-morning song (see examples on pages 14–15).

Warm-Up

Figure out the best way to use your space to perform a running workout. Run in a circle around the spots where the children sit. If space is limited, run in place. Encourage exaggerated arm movements and raising the knees up high.

ACTIVITY • Stretching

Explain that stretching is like pulling gently on a rubber band. Stretching should not hurt when you do it, but you should feel mild pulling. Stretching is important to prevent muscle injury during sports. Model the following stretches while the class performs them:

- Look up and down, and side to side.

- Shrug your shoulders up and down.

- Bend and flex your wrists.

- Open arms wide out to the side.

- Reach arms up high to the sky.

- Reach one arm across your chest and hold with the other hand; repeat with the other arm.

- Step one foot forward and bend that front knee; repeat with the other leg.

- Hold the wall with one hand and use the other hand to grab and hold your ankle behind you so that your knee is bent. This stretches the quadriceps muscle in the front of the thigh. Repeat with the other leg.

- Touch your toes while gently bending and straightening your knees.

ACTIVITY • Find the Match

Before class, take one half of the sport pictures you prepared and tape them to the wall at various reachable heights around the room. Give each child the other half of one of the pictures. Ask the group to find pictures that match their pictures, to remove them from the wall, and to bring them back to the sitting spots in the circle.

Once all the children have found their matches, go around the circle and ask the children to show what their pictures look like with both halves placed together. Then ask everyone to use creative movement at their spots to show what an athlete who plays that sport does. For instance, a picture of a baseball player may inspire the children to get up and pretend to hold a bat, swing, and hit a ball. A picture of a snowboarder may inspire the children to squat down with their arms out to the side to pretend to snowboard down a mountain.

ACTIVITY • Four Corners

Place a picture of a sport in each corner of the room, with a different sport pictured in each corner. With the group in the middle of your space, call out the name of a sport. Ask the children to walk, hop, skip, or jump to the picture of that sport. Repeat with a different sport.

Winding Down

1   **Back to back**: Find a partner. Sit with your backs together and link your arms by the elbows. Carefully try to stand up.

2   **Feet to feet**: Sit facing a friend with legs out straight and feet touching. Try to lift your feet into the air together. Slowly lower feet to the floor.

3   **Find a partner**: You and your partner both make X-shapes with your arms. Lift up your arms with palms open and fingers wide, and give a high five to your partner by tapping palms together. Then lower your arms, maintaining the X shape.

4   **Group cheer**: Stand in a tight, shoulder-to-shoulder circle, and stack all hands on top of one another. Count to three and do a cheer.

Lesson 23 *Pre-Soccer Skills*

I prefer to be outdoors for soccer skills and will wait for a good weather forecast to do so. This can also be done in a large gym area.

Supplies

* one multipurpose ball per child
* cones with colored flags (Saying, "Go to the yellow flag," is more efficient than telling children to go to the "right" or "left" corner.)
* orange or blue painter's tape
* red Stop sign, green Go sign, and yellow Slow sign

Getting Started

Use tape to mark where you want the children to line up. Flags can be made by securing a piece of rectangular felt to a hardware store dowel. Push the dowel into the ground or insert it inside a cone so that the flag is above the top of the cone.

Warm-Up

Gather your group and jog around the space, using the cones to define the four corners of the space. Keep jogging until about half of the children start to slow down or complain that they are getting tired. Scientific method? No, but it works.

Gather and stretch. Perform the following easy standing stretches:

- Reach up to the sky, then down to toes; repeat.

- Stretch arms out to sides and make circles with arms forward and backward.

- Shrug shoulders up and down.

- Rise onto tiptoes, then lower feet back down to the floor; repeat five times.

- Open and close legs. You can turn this into jumping jacks if your group is ready to advance their skill level.

- Stand with legs spread comfortably apart, and bend down to touch the right foot with the left hand. Stand up, then bend down to touch the left foot with the right hand.

- Extend one leg in front and lift up the toes of that foot, keeping the soles of both feet on floor. (This is a hamstring stretch and balance activity.)

ACTIVITY • Ball Skills

Each child gets a ball. Tell the children to place their ball at their feet and wait for instructions. Demonstrate and ask the students if they can do the following:

- put their foot on the ball

- put their heel on the ball. Switch legs and repeat.

- put toes of one foot on the ball. Switch feet and repeat.

- put their elbow on the ball

- sit on the ball

- place both knees on the ball

ACTIVITY • Learning to Dribble

"Watch me first." Demonstrate and say, "Little kick, little kick." Stop the ball.

Now have the children practice. Remind the group that it's not a race. The children should use little kicks to slowly move the ball to the other side of the field or space.

This is easier to do on grass because it slows down the ball. On a smooth gym floor, the children will chase after their balls a lot more, and that will leave less time for skill development.

ACTIVITY • Red Light and Green Light

Revisit the stoplight game. The children already know what to do if you did lesson 1.

Instruct the class that when they see the Go sign, they need to use little kicks to move the ball toward you. When they see the Stop sign, have the younger children stop and sit on the ball. Challenge older children by asking them to stop and balance one foot on the ball when you show the red sign and say, "Stop."

ACTIVITY • Big Kicks

Let's look at opposites in movement. Practicing little kicks is complete. Now it's time to let the class loose, if space allows.

Line up the children horizontally across your space with their balls at their feet. On a count, ask them to kick their balls as hard as they can into the field and watch them go. Once all balls are on the field, the children run to collect them.

Winding Down

Repeat the warm-up's stretching routine; sing a goodbye song (for example, see "Winding Down" in lesson 1 on page 28).

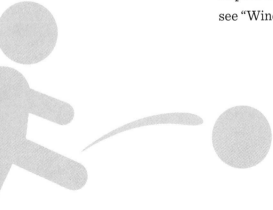

Lesson 24 *Beginning Tennis Skills*

The activities in this lesson showcase foundational large-motor movements required for tennis, not the detailed coordination of hitting a ball with a racket.

Supplies

- paper plate rackets
- trainer tennis balls
- one regular tennis ball
- one tennis racket
- painter's tape
- balloons

Getting Started

Sing a good-morning song (see examples on pages 14–15).

Take some time to talk about tennis. A simple explanation of the game itself and what you use in the game builds a foundation of understanding. Not all children are naturally sports-minded, nor do all families introduce sports into their children's lives.

Show a tennis racket and ask if the class knows what it is. "Yes, a tennis racket."

What is *this* called? Show a tennis ball and say, "a tennis ball."

What is special about this ball? Affirm their response with, "Yes, watch how it bounces."

Show the class the balls you will be using. Tell the children that if they have a tennis lesson, these are the balls they likely will use.

Warm-Up

Start with standing-arm activities.

Arm circles: Move arms outstretched to the sides. Make small circles in the air with your arms.

Elbow to knee: Stand and touch right elbow to your left knee. Demonstrate, and don't worry if your students confuse right and left.

Side stretches: Reach hands up and over your head. Reach a little to one side while arms are still up. Then reach to the other side.

Sweep the floor: Stand and stretch your arms above your head. Then reach your arms to touch the floor, keeping your knees straight. Gently swing your arms from side to side in a sweeping motion.

ACTIVITY • Touch and Go Drills

Tape lines of various lengths on the gym floor with painter's tape. Have time to get fancy? Use different colors of tape. The different colors will help the children follow your instructions.

Mark a start line, then mark another line five feet across the floor from it, another line eight to ten feet away, and so on, depending on the space available.

Be sure to demonstrate these directions as you're saying them: "When I say, 'One, two, three, go,' you run to the first blue [or specify a different color] line and bend down to touch it. Then run back to the start line. When I say, 'go' again, run to the second [or say the color] line."

This elementary school drill translates well into a preschool movement class.

ACTIVITY • Shuffling

Demonstrate and verbalize how to shuffle sideways along the classroom space. Verbal cue: "Step and slide." Repeat a few times.

ACTIVITY • Paper Plate Rackets

My homemade paper plate rackets lasted almost five years before I had to replace some of them. Take a thick paper plate and cut two parallel lines in the middle. Get free, medium-size paint sticks at a hardware store. Slide sticks into the plate, and you have a racket. Use packing tape to secure the sticks along the cut lines to give the racket more longevity.

Give each child a paper plate racket. Show the children how they will roll their balls across the floor with their rackets. Instruct them to keep the balls as close to themselves as possible, using the words *with control*.

Regroup. Try to balance the ball on the plate while holding the racket handle.

Challenge

If half or more of the group has mastered the skill, ask all children to balance the ball on top of the paper plate racket while walking across the floor.

ACTIVITY • Paper Plate Rackets and Balloons

This is a great coordination activity that develops pre-tennis skill by focusing on connecting the racket with the target. In this activity, the target is a balloon.

"We will each be getting a balloon. When you get your balloon, just hold it and wait until everyone has a balloon. When I say, 'go,' try to gently hit your balloon with your racket."

"What could we do to protect our friends? Yes, we can watch our bubbles, or spaces, to make sure we are tapping only our balloons."

Challenge

If half or more of the group manages this skill well, try a challenge by introducing a net. Use two cones with orange masking tape attached to each and stretch the tape across the class space. Divide the class into partner pairs and give each pair one balloon. Tell the children to tap the balloon over the tape to their partners. This can be hectic in a larger group, depending on your group dynamics. Try it, and you can always switch to a different activity or to closure, as needed. Having additional adults available for supervision promotes a more successful activity.

Winding Down

Pick a coordination song or task.

- Perform the upper-body portion of the Brain Gym hook-up task (Dennison and Dennison 2010). Extend your arms out to the side, move thumbs up, thumbs down, tap the back of your hands together, interlace your fingers, and bend your elbows to bring your clasped hands to your chest.

- Stretch arms out to the side, then hug yourself and say, "I love me." Repeat with the other arm on top.

- Sing a goodbye song (for example, see "Winding Down" in lesson 1 on page 28).

Lesson 25 **Beginning Volleyball**

You may notice this lesson's similarity to previous lessons. Redundancy builds motor memory and boosts self-esteem as children recognize skills they have already practiced.

Supplies

- volleyball
- balloons
- spots
- net, painter's tape, or cones with rope

Getting Started

Start by sitting in a circle. Without talking, blow up a balloon with a bit of dramatic gusto, then release it so that it deflates and whizzes around the room. There's about a 90 percent certainty that the class's attention is now captured.

Show pictures of a volleyball or verbally describe what one looks like. Briefly compare and contrast it with other balls.

Reminder: Just a simple explanation of the game will suffice. Talk about how groups of people stand on either side of a tall net and hit the ball with their hands to the other team.

Even soft trainer volleyballs can be hard on the hands. Using balloons is the best way to start.

Warm-Up

Volleyball requires arm strength and coordination. Try these selected warm-ups to build both. Start sitting.

- Wake up body: Gently tap or touch your neck, shoulders, arms, and legs.
- Spider fingers: Sit with legs crossed. Crawl your fingers on the floor in front of your body as far as you can reach with your bottom on the floor. Then crawl your fingers back. Repeat, crawling your fingers to the right, then the left sides of your body.

- Crab lifts: Sit with knees bent in front and feet on floor in front of you. Place hands behind, palms on floor. Lift your bottom off the floor. Hold briefly. Drop your bottom back to the floor. Repeat.

- Stomp it out, loud and soft: Sit with knees bent and feet on floor in front of you. Alternating legs, lift feet up and down to stomp them on the floor. Stomp loudly. Then tiptoe stomp softly. Repeat. Always end with soft stomping before moving on to the next activity.

ACTIVITY • Floating Children

Set up the activity while talking about the difference between air- and helium-filled balloons.

- "I filled up my balloon with air from my mouth."

- "What if I filled it up with another gas, called helium?"

- "What would the balloon do?"

- "Have you seen birthday party balloons float?"

- "Let's pretend to fill ourselves up with helium and float around the room."

- "When I touch your head (or make a sound) and call out your name, you will pop and float to the floor."

- "After you float to the floor, please wait there until all the balloons have been popped."

ACTIVITY • Group Balloon

Gather the group in a standing circle. Hold hands. "We are going to be a huge balloon. Let's walk into the middle of the circle and get as close as we can. It's important to try to keep holding hands. Let's blow ourselves up and pretend to blow air into our large balloon."

As the children gently purse their lips and blow air, slowly step backward until everyone's arms are completely outstretched. Then pop yourselves and gently fall to the floor. You'll see many smiles with this activity.

ACTIVITY • Free Play with Balloons

Set a timer for five minutes or less and allow the children to explore what they can do with their balloons. Recommendation: Use the same color balloons to avoid conflicts.

ACTIVITY • Volleyball with Balloons

Set up a low net. On a budget? Use rope and cones, painter's tape and cones, or painter's tape in a line on the floor. If your group needs guidance to stay on their team's side, taking the preparatory time to mark off individual spots will be well worth the effort. I learned that the hard way.

Divide the class into groups of two and ask the pairs to tap a balloon gently back and forth to each other.

Winding Down

Group chant: Show the class what a team will do. Gather in a close circle and chant the class name or say loudly, "Go, team!"

Lesson 26 *Beginner Baseball*

Warning: this lesson requires a lot of setup and is best done in a large, safe space.

Supplies

- large cones
- foam bats
- beanbags
- wall-hanging target
- blankets
- bases (store-bought or yoga mat pieces)
- large Wiffle balls

Getting Started

Talk about the shape of a baseball field being a diamond. Place bases on the available floor space in a diamond shape. Show the bat and the ball used in baseball. Allow the children to touch a real baseball if available and pass it around the group as you talk about the game.

Explain that you will use Wiffle balls for safety because a real baseball is very hard and could hurt. Pretend to hit a ball with a bat, and then demonstrate running the bases.

Warm-Up

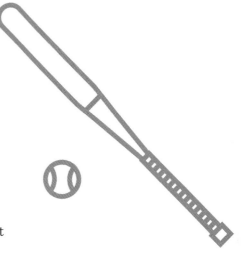

- Shake hands high, shake hands low.

- Open and close legs while standing.

- Open arms to the side and then shut them.

- Do jumping jacks.

- Give yourself a hug.

- Make arm circles in the air out to the side.

- Draw figure eights. Clasp hands together and draw a big 8 in the air. Having a piece of paper nearby with a picture of the numeral 8 will assist your visual learners.

- Paint rainbows in the sky. Clasp hands together, pretend to hold a large paintbrush, and dip it into a bucket of paint at your side. Arch hands upward, drawing a rainbow. Each time you make an arch, allow a child to say the color he wants the class to paint.

- Stretch quadriceps. Lie on the belly or on one side and try to hold your ankle so that your knee is bent. Hold for twenty seconds if possible, then switch legs.

- Grow bigger, bigger, and jump.

ACTIVITY • Baseball Stations

Stations are helpful for direct observation of motor skills and allow for one-on-one instruction. One teacher or adult per station helps the flow and focus.

- **Batting practice**: Set up four or five cones and place a Wiffle ball on top of each one. Have a foam bat at each station. Mark and verbalize clearly where the children should stand and in which direction they should swing the bat to hit the ball. It's helpful to use a taped X on the floor to show the children where to stand next to the cone.

If a child is left-handed, it's easy to switch the cone to the other side of the X to hit the ball. Try not to demonstrate or promote batting on a specific side. Let the children experiment with left- or right-handed batting. "Try it this way." "What feels easier?"

For safety, it's important to have the children stay in their spots while batting. You can run down the lines and replace balls as they are hit to encourage the group to stay on the X. When all balls have been used, the bats stay by the cones while the children gather the balls and put them back into your bucket.

- **Throwing station**: Designate the space to be used. Be sure to tape off boundaries showing where everyone should stand. Remind the class to stay in that area so that no one is throwing and retrieving at the same time. Chaos is more likely to occur without having proper setup and guidance already in place.

  Marking boundaries minimizes having to say no to the group. Children lose an opportunity to develop self-awareness when negative language like *no* is used or when cooperation is forced (Lasater and Lasater 2009; Stiffelman 2012). You can say, "Please stand on the taped line," as a positive way to encourage participation. Use a target along a wall, with blankets or a rug placed under the target to limit the number of balls that roll away.

  As long as the group stay somewhere inside the designated taped space, allow the children to throw at their leisure. Instead of lining up to throw one by one, they can take one ball at a time from the bucket, throw, and keep going until the balls run out. This allows those who have mastered throwing to go at their own pace while others can acquire practice slowly. With supervision, this activity is very successful, and the children appreciate the freedom within the structure.

- **Run the bases**: If you have the space and assistance, try this as a separate station with a small group. If you don't have these resources, you can do it as a group activity with the entire class. Ideally, use a grassy outdoor space.

  One child at a time will take a foam bat, step up to home plate, and pretend to hit a ball. As each child runs around the bases, encourage the group to call out, "First, second, third, *home!*" as loudly as they can. (This introduces math skills.) Cheer, and the next child steps up to bat.

  Why pretend? Why not just hit a ball? A ball tee could be used, but think about who is in your group. If more than half of the children find this activity intimidating because they are still developing this motor skill, then keep it simple. Your goal is to increase self-esteem and have fun while learning the basics of this sport.

- **Throw and catch (challenge station):** Designate spaces for partners to stand. Have each pair throw a foam ball back and forth.

     Verbal cues to thrower: "Hold ball in one hand up by your ear, step forward with opposite leg, throw, and let go." "Be sure that your partner is ready. Try calling out your partner's name before you throw."

     Verbal cues to catcher: "Hands open and out in front. Be ready. Keep your eyes on the ball."

Winding Down

Gather in a small circle and chant your class name or say a generic, "Go, team!"

Lesson 27 *Beginning Tae Kwon Do*

I included this lesson as an example that you can pick any sport or activity and teach the basics. I am not a black belt—or any belt, for that matter. First, summarize martial arts from your research or personal experience. For example, you can say, "Karate originated in Okinawa, Japan, and has a focus on hand movements. Tae kwon do originated in Korea and has more foot techniques. These are just two examples of types of martial arts." I make a point to tell my group that I am not a master martial artist and that we are learning together.

Supplies

- foam balls
- cones
- mat
- balance beam

Getting Started

Giving children opportunities to spend time in bare feet is a way to build motor control and supports sensory development in their feet. Therefore, I encourage you to perform this lesson with bare feet.

Questions for the class: "What is respect?" "What do you do to show respect?" Sample answers: Say, "Please," and "Thank you," or listen.

"Respect is important in tae kwon do, and we will focus on respect, humility, perseverance, self-control, and honesty. There are ways we can show respect in martial arts, such as bowing. Feet together, hands at your sides, and bow." I've seen different variations on the five tenets of tae kwon do, so please do your research and decide what you want to present.

Try bowing toward a friend by facing each other, hands at your sides, and leaning forward slightly.

Warm-Up

Try marching or running in one place to warm up all the muscles. I recommend about one to two minutes. Observe your children for signs of fatigue, and stop before they lose interest.

Sit down. Use touch to stimulate proprioception in their feet. Ask your students to gently rub or tap the bottoms and tops of their feet for one minute.

ACTIVITY • Basic Tae Kwon Do Postures

- **Attention stance**: stand with feet together, arms hanging down on each side of your body.
- **Ready stance**: stand with feet apart, hands closed into fists in front of your body.
- **Forward stance**: stand with one leg forward with knee bent and rear leg straight. Rear arm is bent and forward arm is straight in front of the body, pointing either down or forward.
- **Standing balance**: stand on one leg.
- **Front kick**: lift one foot off the floor and kick it forward.
- **Side kick**: lift one foot off the floor and kick it to the side.
- **Blocking stance**: hold arms in front of your body with elbows bent and in front of your face.

Use pictures, demonstrations, and verbal instructions for each posture to target all learning styles.

Challenge

Call out and demonstrate postures. Then mix up the order. Move quickly between postures. Then try calling out postures verbally without demonstration. "Attention: forward, ready, front kick," and so on.

ACTIVITY • Tae Kwon Do Stations

Keep the time frame short at each supervised station to keep the children's attention and for their safety. This activity is also great for doing at home.

- **Somersault on a mat**: Squat with hands in front of you on a mat. Tuck head and chin down. Push off feet. Roll forward and over.

- **Kick foam balls off cones**: Place foam balls on short cones, with one child per cone for safety. Ask the children to try to kick the balls off the cones. Use space safely.

- **Jump over a balance beam**: Initially, use a balance beam or equivalent that is soft and close to the floor for safety. Ask the children to take turns jumping over the beam.

Winding Down

Being able to pause and breathe is an important part of martial arts.

Sit cross-legged on the floor. "Let's all close our eyes. Slowly breathe in through your nose. Breathe out through your mouth. Try to get quiet and not worry about what your friend is doing next to you."

One minute is just enough time for focused breathing. After a minute, some of your children will want to stay quiet while others will start to squirm.

Challenge
Jump sideways over a beam or piece of foam.

CHAPTER 9
Pick-Your-Theme Lesson Plans

The following lessons are based on different topics and combine various activities and milestones while at the same time incorporating a specific topic. Themes can be based on shapes, seasons, animals, or numbers.

Lesson 28 *Playing with Circles*

I hope this lesson inspires you to add movement to your curriculum for learning about shapes.

Supplies

- sitting spots
- beanbags
- hoops

Getting Started

Talk about shapes. Look around the room and ask your students to identify different shapes. Example statements: "I see a circle in the ceiling light" or "I see a rectangular door."

Warm-Up

Sing the song, "The Wheels on the Bus."

ACTIVITY • Beanbags

Have your group sit in a circle or a line, depending on the space available. Just be sure that all the children can see you. Each child gets a beanbag. I like to make my own. It's not too difficult to do, plus, it's better for your budget.

Then say, "Do as I do":

- Balance the beanbag on your hand.

- Balance it on your shoulder.

- Balance it on your head.

- Stand up with it on your head. "See what happens."

- Balance it on top of your foot.

- Balance it on top of your other foot.

- Try standing on one leg. Then try the other leg. Sometimes, modeling placing one foot on top of the other foot is easier than lifting the knee up high.

- Lift toes up and tap them on the floor a few times.

- Lift heels up and down a few times.

ACTIVITY • Free Play with Hoops

Talk about the shape of the hoops as they are being passed out. "What shape is this? Is it a square? Is it a diamond? Is it a circle?" Allow exploration time. About five to seven minutes of free play until the next activity is a good start. Monitor the children to see if they want more time or need less time. When is less time needed? When half of the group loses sight of the instructions by running around or not monitoring personal bubbles.

ACTIVITY • Let's Try It with Hoops

We will see all the things we can do with a hoop. Say, "Try it; see what happens":

- Walk through the hoop.

- Twirl it on your arm.

- Twirl it around your waist.

- Spin the hoop on its side.

- Swing it on your arm, then on your other arm.

- Swing it on your leg.

- Put the hoop on the floor and throw a beanbag into it.

ACTIVITY • Ring-around-the-Rosy

Place a large hoop on the floor. Stand in a circle around the hoop, hold hands, walk in a circle, and sing "Ring-around-the-Rosy." When you say the word *down*, everyone lets go of hands and sits. Sing with a regular tempo. Sing with a slow tempo. Then try a fast tempo as you walk quickly around in a circle.

Ring around the rosy, pocket full of posies,

Ashes, ashes, we all fall down!

Winding Down

This is an English or Scottish folksong from circa 1912. Be sure to be a role model by moving in parallel with the movement words. March in place at the beginning of the song.

Hold hands in a circle and lift arms up with the word *up*.

Squat at the word *down* and lift arms only halfway up when you say, "halfway up."

The grand old Duke of York,
He had ten thousand men.
He marched them up to the top of the hill,
He marched them down again.
And when they're up, they're up.
And when they're down, they're down.
And when they're only halfway up,
They're neither up nor down.

If you want to add a little equity, sing a new version, "Grand Old Duchess of York."

Lesson 29 *"Let It Snow" and "Let's Ice-Skate"*

This lesson is a favorite during the winter months, especially if you live in a climate that may limit outdoor playtime due to cold temperatures.

Supplies

- sitting spots
- scarves
- wax paper cut into foot-size rectangles

Getting Started

Children enjoy being active participants. Ask them what ice and snow feel like. Ask them if they've seen or visited an ice-skating rink. Show them a picture of an ice-skater.

Warm-Up

Every so often after working with the same group of children for a while, I skip the introduction and go right into the warm-up. This is especially true if a class is running late or I know it will take more time to complete an activity.

- Do a crossing midline activity: "Twist into a pretzel."
- While standing, point and flex feet.
- Open and close legs.
- Sit on the floor and bend knees. Alternate lifting legs up, then lift both legs into a V pose.
- Sit on the floor, place hands behind you on the floor, bend knees, and lift bottom up for crab position. Count out loud, "One, two, three," then drop bottom down onto the floor.
- Get on all fours and kneel with hands on the floor.
- Perform cat and cow poses. Kneeling with hands on the floor, arch the back upward while you look down. Then arch your belly toward the floor as you look up.
- Lie on your belly for pretend sledding. Lift arms and legs briefly, hold that position, return to lying on the belly, and rest. Repeat.

ACTIVITY • Let It Snow

It's free-dance-with-scarves time. Pick a winter song like Dean Martin's "Let It Snow, Let It Snow, Let It Snow" (1966). It's always important to be culturally sensitive and choose a generic song that is appropriate for all people.

If you don't have scarves, make snowflakes out of paper and let the children dance with them instead. If you work in a setting in which the class comes to you for a movement lesson, an option would be for you to make the snowflakes before class. Otherwise, cutting out snowflakes can be incorporated into your lesson as a fine-motor task, followed by the big-movement actions of dancing.

ACTIVITY • Snow People

Now that there is pretend snow (paper snowflakes) all over the floor, it's time to show the class how to make snow people. Lying on the floor in the "snow," open and close your legs and arms at the same time.

ACTIVITY • Trek to the Ice Rink

Tell your students that it's time to line up and look to the horizon. Tell them they will be trekking through huge piles of snow that their legs can slowly sink into.

Demonstrate, then do together: lunges. Yes, lunges. You know, those exercises where you first step with one leg forward, then drop the rear knee to touch the ground, and repeat on the other side.

Verbal cues: "Step, touch back knee," or simply say, "Step, touch."

Make the trip to the rink fun by stopping to jump over a crevasse. A *crevasse* is a deep, open crack in a glacier or the earth. "Can you say *crevasse*?" "Now, jump!"

Some groups can make a series of small jumps to go back and forth across a ten-foot space a few times. Do not underestimate what your group can do. Remember, you are doing it too, to the best of your ability, and that is the best example.

ACTIVITY • Ice Skating

Use wax paper cut into rectangles about the size of a preschooler's shoe. Just as when learning to ice skate, always keep both feet on the floor during this activity. First, place a piece of wax paper under each foot. Slide across a smooth floor (a rug will not work). Remind the children that skating is not walking, but sliding.

Music: A slow waltz or other slow music will encourage the sliding steps required to do this task. It's also calming and will encourage the children's focus.

Tip: Show your children that another way to slide is with just one foot on wax paper and the other foot pushing off from the floor. This is a good tip if they find that wax paper under each foot is too slippery or difficult.

Challenge

Children can be pulled gently if they plant both feet on wax paper. They can try turning or gliding or spinning on their wax "skates."

Winding Down

Pick any winter song below. My favorite is the last song listed because the students can take the wax paper they skated on and crumple it to make snowballs. The children line up in a row and sing the song. When the song says, "Throw it now," have all the children throw their snowballs at you. Collect the paper snowballs and discard.

"It's Winter and You Know It" (Sung to the tune of "If You're Happy and You Know It.")

It is winter and it's time to ride a sled.
It is winter and it's time to ride a sled.
It is winter, that's the season.
We don't need a better reason.
It is winter and it's time to ride a sled.

"You Put Your Right Mitten In" (Sung to the tune of "The Hokey Pokey.")

You put your right mitten in,
You take your right mitten out.
You put your right mitten in, and you shake it all about.
You do the winter pokey, and you turn yourself around.
That's what it's all about!

Repeat with new lines:

You put your left mitten in . . .
You put your right boot . . .
You put your left boot . . .

You put your winter hat in . . .
You put your snowsuit (or whole body) in . . .

"Dance Like Snowflakes" (Sung to the tune of "Frère Jacques.")

Dance like snowflakes, dance like snowflakes,
In the air, in the air.
Whirling, twirling snowflakes.
Whirling, twirling snowflakes.
Here and there, here and there.

"Make a Snowball" (Sung to the tune of "Frère Jacques.")

Make a snowball, make a snowball.
Throw it now, throw it now.
Make a snowball, make a snowball.
Throw it now, throw it now.

Lesson 30 *Using Hands for Support*

If I could pick the most important lesson for supporting prewriting skills, this is it! Children need more opportunities to build upper arm and shoulder strength. Raising their arms above their heads and using their arms to crawl is a good start.

Supplies

• construction paper handprints

Getting Started

Sit in a circle. Start with a brief discussion about all the things you can do with your hands. You can draw, paint, open doors, brush hair, or scratch an itch.

Warm-Up

Sing a good-morning song (see examples on pages 14–15).

ACTIVITY • Handprints Along the Wall

Take handprints cut from construction paper and tape them along a wall at points both higher and lower than the average preschooler's height.

The children line up and walk along the wall, tapping the handprints with their open palms. This promotes upper-body strengthening because it takes muscle endurance to maintain your hands at or above shoulder height during the length of time it takes to walk along the wall. This, in turn, builds the shoulder complex's musculature and helps with prewriting skills.

I thought this might not be worth the effort of cutting out all those handprints and could be boring after one walk down the wall. But I was surprised by how easily the children became interested in it, enjoyed it, and kept running back to the end of the line to try it again.

ACTIVITY • Building Arm Strength

Building arm strength, specifically in the shoulder, requires weight-bearing activities that involve the hands. The shoulder muscles are the foundation of support for handwriting skills. Without a stable base of support in the shoulder girdle, it can be difficult to develop handwriting endurance and good writing technique. You may see an example of a lack of shoulder strength when a child flops over a desk while writing. It may also manifest itself in a student's poor grasp of a pencil. Sensory feedback children get while using their hands for locomotion encourages motor skill development for writing. Try these tasks:

- **Crab walk**: With bellies up and hands behind you on the floor, walk on hands and feet to the other side of the room.

- **Bear walk**: On hands and feet, bend over in a V position and walk to the other side of the room.

- **Inchworm walk**: Lying on belly, pull body forward with arms. Then squirm bottom and legs forward; repeat.

- **Donkey kicks**: Stand with hands flat on the floor in front so that you are leaning over with your bottom pointing up. Kick one leg up off the floor into the air and return that leg to stand on the floor. Try with the other leg. Repeat.

Challenge

Wheelbarrow walk. Divide class into pairs. One child in each pair places his palms on the floor in front of his body. His partner stands behind him, picks up his feet, and holds the feet at hip level. The pair then walks forward, with the child in front walking only on his hands.

Winding Down

Lie on bellies, with forearms and hands underneath the torso. This creates some gentle back extension and is a modified cobra pose.

Sing a favorite song in this position. Some children may start to say their arms are sore from the combination of activities in this lesson. Most of us don't normally use our arms for any type of weight-bearing activity.

Song idea 1: "Rub Your Hands (Om Song)" (Karma Kids Yoga 2008). *"Rub your hands, sit up tall, take a deep breath, om."* This verse repeats again and again so that you can sing a few verses while the children are on their bellies, continue singing as the children push up into a taller cobra pose on the verse "sit up tall," and then transition into a sitting position to complete the song while sitting.

Song idea 2: Sit in a circle and sing "Clap Your Hands" (They Might Be Giants 2005). This is a high-energy, fast-transition song.

Lesson 31 *Move like Animals*

My students love watching me move like a monkey or hop like a frog! It's a novelty to see an adult move like an animal. So use that to your advantage to engage your group. Bonus: this lesson is easy to set up.

Supplies

- pictures of animals or stuffed animals
- painter's tape or balance beam

Getting Started

Spend a few minutes in the opening circle with the children sitting on their spots. Discuss how they got to class that day. How did they get to the movement classroom? How do people get somewhere? *Walk, run, hop, jump, skip, drive in a car, ride a bicycle...*

How do animals get places? For example: Frogs? Kangaroos? Dogs? Cats?

Warm-Up

- Take-5 breathe.

- Point and flex feet while in a long sit.

- Sit cross-legged on floor. Walk spider fingers away from your body and back, to the right side and back, to the left side and back, and behind you and back while the chest lifts up.

- Do trunk rolls. Sit with knees bent in front and hands on the floor in back for support. Keeping knees together, rock them to touch the floor on one side of the body, then to the other side.

- Be a merry-go-round. Sit with knees bent in front, and turn around and around in circles using feet and hands.

ACTIVITY • Move Like Animals

Clearly mark your space to maintain the group's focus and to minimize verbal reminders and redirection.

Place pictures of animals or stuffed animals at each station to provide a visual cue.

Split the group into equal-size smaller groups so that all can take turns. Use a sliding whistle or other sound to signal when time is up at stations and groups should rotate to new stations.

Kangaroo hop: Mark two parallel lines on the floor. Children stand on one line and practice jumping to the parallel line.

Cheetah run: Run back and forth along a length of at least ten to fifteen feet. Make it interesting by asking runners to hold a stuffed toy cheetah while running, and to pass it to the next child when they return to the start line.

Balance beam monkey walk: I use a sturdy plastic balance beam set. If you don't have a budget for a beam, use colored tape on the floor. Monkeys climb trees and walk with their knees bent. Walk along the beam by sidestepping. Then walk along the beam heel to toe, placing one foot directly in front of the other.

Challenge

Using a spotter (someone to catch a child who starts to fall), have the children try walking backward along the balance beam.

Winding Down

Greg and Steve had a mob of teacher fans at a conference I attended in Washington, DC. They really do have great songs. "Animal Action 1" and "Animal Action 2" are on their *Kids in Motion* CD (1987).

No setup is required. Play the song and demonstrate the moves as you and the children follow the instructions given in the song.

Children enjoy seeing a teacher be the student by listening and doing the lyrics with the group. Maybe even making a mistake or two. When children see adults make mistakes, it gives them permission to make mistakes and learn.

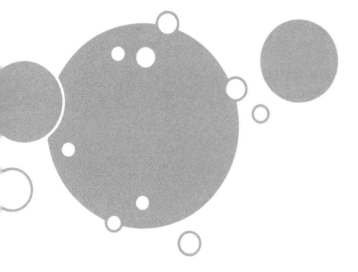

CHAPTER 10
Let's-Play-a-Game Lesson Plans

Sometimes we just want to play. The focus of the next five lessons is to have fun while indirectly learning an academic concept, such as counting numbers, sequencing tasks, or identifying a number's written name.

Lesson 32 *Number Games*

We move, and we learn. Adding numbers to your games is easy. "Four Corners" gets the children excited as they process what number is called out and where to go. If you have a large group, be careful to play in a large space to maintain safety. "Count the Chairs" practices the ability to recognize numbers. The parachute activity with large dice combines aerobic effort with counting out loud.

Supplies

- sitting spots
- one beanbag
- four cones
- chairs
- sticky notes
- parachute
- foam dice (if available)

Getting Started

Sing a welcome song and follow with an easy icebreaker. Toss a beanbag to a child in the opening circle and ask them to catch it, say their name, and throw it back to you. Repeat for each child.

Warm-Up

Sit or stand with legs crossed. Extend arms out to the side with thumbs pointing down. Keeping thumbs pointing down, cross arms in front of you into an X. Bend elbows and bring crossed arms next to your chest. Hold for a few seconds. Repeat twice (Dennison and Dennison 2010). Then do a few of your favorite stretches and activities from the warm-up samples in appendix B.

ACTIVITY • Four Corners with Numbers

Label each of four cones with a different number from one to four, and place one cone in each of the four corners of your space. Gather the children in a large group. Call out a number and ask the group to walk to the cone that has that number. Once the children understand the concept, ask them to run, crawl, skip, or hop to the designated cone with each number that you call out.

ACTIVITY • Count the Chairs

Prepare one chair per child in your class. Line up chairs and write a number on a sticky note; do not write the same number on more than one sticky note. Place one sticky note on the back of each chair. Ask the children to keep walking around the line of chairs while music is playing. When the music stops, the children stop walking, find a chair, and sit on it. Once all are seated, ask them to tell you what number is on their chair. Restart the music, and while the class is walking to the music, reorder the numbers on the chairs. Repeat.

An alternative is to give each child a sticker with a unique number, in addition to numbering the chairs. When the music stops, children need to look for the chair with a number that corresponds to their sticker. (See lesson 33 for a variation of this activity.)

ACTIVITY • Toss the Dice

If you have access to a parachute and foam dice, ask the children to hold the edge of the parachute. Put the dice in the center of the parachute. Shake the edges of the parachute until the dice fall onto the floor. Ask the children to count the number of dots they see face-up on the dice. Repeat.

Winding Down

Sing a goodbye song (for example, see "Winding Down" in lesson 1 on page 28).

Lesson 33 *Copycat and Musical Chairs*

If you are looking for a lesson to learn about your students' capabilities, pick this one. Copycat allows you to demonstrate a motor skill and then observe what they can do. Make notes and find other lessons that reinforce the skills that need more practice.

The preschool teachers I work with like the musical chair twist using names. This game helps identify the students they can support in learning how their names look in writing.

Supplies

- sitting spots or chairs for each child
- sticky notes
- music

Getting Started

"It's all about fun games today. You will be watching how to move your body and learning how to recognize your written name."

Warm-Up

Promote upper-body strength.

- Take-5 breathe: breathe in for a count of five, and out for a count of five.

- Cow and cat pose: get on all fours with hands and knees on the floor. Drop the belly down to the floor while you raise your head to look up. Arch your back and look down toward your belly. Repeat a few times.

- Downward-facing dog pose: on hands and knees, walk hands forward until belly touches the floor, then walk hands backward into downward-facing dog pose.

- Snake pose: lie on your belly, rest your upper body on your forearms, and hiss like a snake. Rest your entire body on the floor; raise your upper body on forearms. Repeat twice.

- Crab lift: sit with knees bent in front and hands on the floor behind you; lift your bottom off the floor. Sing a song or count down, "Five, four, three, two, one, zero," to encourage children to maintain this position.

- Squat: stand with feet on the floor, knees bent, and your bottom low but not touching the floor.

- Jump: squat and say, "Getting bigger, bigger, jump!" as the children gradually stand up straight and jump vertically.

ACTIVITY • Copycat

It's time to get the group's attention. If you have a pair of cat ears, place them on your head. This is a copycat game that is easy and engaging and allows the children to try multiple motor skills.

Perform some type of action and ask the children to copy you. Jump up and down and ask the group, "Can you jump up and down?" Quickly move to another action: "Can you spin in a circle?" "Can you tap the top of your head?" "Can you stand on one foot?" "Can you stand on tiptoe?"

If you run out of ideas, ask another teacher to be the cat. Give the cat ears to them and ask the group to follow their actions. A different leader will diversify the actions the class can mimic.

ACTIVITY • Musical Chairs

This is a noncompetitive version of musical chairs. Both students and teachers have fun with this game. It's a great time of dancing without a child getting excluded. Plus, it gives the children practice in learning to recognize the written form of their names.

Line up chairs in a long row. Place a sticky-note name tag on each chair, one name tag for each child in the group.

Say, "When you hear the music start, walk or dance in a line around the chairs. Watch me. When the music stops, stop walking and dancing, try to find the chair with your name on it, and sit on that chair."

My favorite song to use for this activity is "Happy" (Williams 2013).

Challenge

Once 90 percent of the group can find their name tags easily and sit on the chairs to the cue of music stopping, increase the challenge. Lead the children briefly away from the chairs and ask them to count to fifteen with their eyes closed. You can also ask the group to try ten jumping jacks. Let them know that they will go back to the musical chair game when they are done. While the children are distracted, move name tags to different chairs.

Resume the musical chair game. When the music stops, the children look for their name tags and sit on the appropriate chairs. The children should figure out that their name tags are now on different chairs.

If you need a greater challenge for your group, involve your helpers. Have them turn some of the chairs to face different directions during a brief distraction break. After the break, the children will need to figure out how to access the chair with their name after the music stops.

Winding Down: Sing a Make-Me-Giggle Song

Use the song "Tootie Ta (Tooty Tot)" (Johnny Only 2012).

There are multiple versions of this classic song. It's also one of those songs that gets stuck in your head all day. Dance to this action song with extra gusto, and make it silly and fun.

Lesson 34 *Four Corners, Push and Pull, and Parachute*

This lesson is best after trying other movement lessons or with a class that has been together.

I dare you to try the "Push and Pull" challenge and see what happens! Children feel empowered and confident after this activity.

Supplies

- sitting spots
- four orange safety cones
- big sturdy boxes or laundry baskets
- several blankets
- parachute
- one or more foam balls

Getting Started

Use the song "Clap Your Hands" (They Might Be Giants 2005).

Warm-Up

Sit in a circle and do the following:

- Point and flex feet.
- Open and close legs.
- Count down. Walk fingers from thighs to toes, saying, "Five, four, three, two, one."
- Perform a snake pose. On bellies, push up onto elbows and make a hissing sound like a snake.
- Fly like a bird. On bellies, with arms and legs spread out like a bird, lift chest and hold position. Repeat.
- Perform cow and cat poses. Get on all fours with hands and knees on the floor. Drop your belly down to the floor while you raise your head to look up. Arch your back and look down toward your belly. Repeat a few times.
- Do a side trunk stretch. Sit cross-legged. Lift arms up, stretch one arm upward and toward the opposite side. Repeat with the other arm and side.

ACTIVITY • Four Corners

In lesson 32 we used cones marked with a number on each one. If you don't have four orange safety cones, use four paper signs. Each sign should be marked with a number (one, two, three, or four) or a color (blue, red, green, or yellow). Tape a numbered or colored paper onto each corner of your space.

Demonstrate and explain. "Watch me first." Redundant phrases like "Watch me first" form helpful habits by automatically cueing the child's attention to instructions. Encourage visual and auditory learning by saying, "Watch me with your eyes" or "Listen with your ears."

Call out a number or color. Ask the children to run carefully to the matching cone and wait for the next cue. Then call out a new number or color from another corner. Repeat until interest or time runs out.

Challenge
Ask the children to hop, skip, or crawl to the corners instead of running.

ACTIVITY • Push and Pull

The ability to push and pull is a coordination skill. It promotes the ability of muscle groups to work together to manipulate an object.

Push boxes: Fill empty mailing boxes or laundry baskets with heavy blocks or with anything that adds five to ten pounds of weight. Group the children into as many lines as the number of boxes. Each child pushes a box across the room, turns, and pushes the box back to the next child in line.

Pull a friend: When I was young, my brother would sit on a blanket and I would pull him across the kitchen floor. Use sturdy blankets for this activity; I use colorful thick ones from Mexico.

Group the children into one team for every blanket you have. If you have three blankets and fifteen children, there will be five children in each of three groups. Demonstrate and explain first.

Spread a blanket on the floor. Ask a child to lie on her back on the blanket, with her feet toward you, the puller. When she is ready, you will grab the edge of the blanket near her feet and pull her across the space. A smooth floor is best for pulling; carpet is less ideal because it creates more drag and effort. Children take turns being pullers and riders.

Challenge
Split your class into teams with one team on either side of the room. One child will push the weighted box across the room to a child from the other team, who then pushes it back. The goal is to practice processing multiple actions of a modified task.

ACTIVITY • Parachute

There are a ton of ideas available for games with parachutes. "Keep it simple" is my motto. Otherwise, your class may get carried away. (Yep, corny pun intended.)

It's always best to start with the group sitting in a circle. This helps assess the children's ability to work together and to be successful with the game. It also helps keep the excitement from becoming disruptive, enhances focus on the intended skills, and builds the students' confidence in team play.

Sit on spots in a large circle. Say, "Everyone, please close your eyes and try not to peek." This small step builds their anticipation and excitement. Spread the parachute on the floor and say, "Open your eyes!"

Each child is instructed to hold a piece or loop of the parachute with their hands.

- **Shake**: Try shaking the parachute gently up and down. Stop. Repeat. Prepare for lots of giggles and smiles.

- **Popcorn**: Add one foam ball to the center of the stationary parachute. Ask the group to try to shake it off, starting on the count of three. "One, two, three, shake." Continue to add more foam balls to increase the complexity. You can add a musical popcorn song during the activity. Try shaking fast, then shake slowly, or try shaking to the tempo of a song. Try the song "Popcorn" (2007).

Once the children can successfully follow instructions with the parachute while they sit, try the same activities while the children stand.

- **Ball pop**: Stand up holding the parachute. Get your group to squat down, then all quickly stand up and at the same time raise their arms upward while holding the parachute. This will briefly create a dome shape. If you add a ball to the center of the parachute, then squat and quickly stand with arms up, the ball should pop straight up into the air.

Winding Down

Refocus for the transition with a Take-5 breathe. Breathe in for a count of "One, two, three, four, five," then breathe out for "One, two, three, four, five."

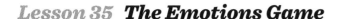

Lesson 35 *The Emotions Game*

During the year, I may notice a conflict arise between some of the students in my classes. When this happens I reach for this lesson.

Supplies

- sitting spots
- individual pictures of several emotions (happy, sad, excited, and tired)
- music

Getting Started

Tense and relax: Begin in a circle. Say, "Show me what tense looks like." They make fists with their hands and scrunch up their faces. "Now show me what relaxed looks like." They may lie on their backs and release their muscles. Alternate calling out "tense" and "relax" a few times.

Warm-Up

Try "Chicken Dance" (The Hit Crew Kids 2013).

ACTIVITY • See, Hear, Touch, and Relate

Seat your group in a circle. Show the children a picture of an emotion (like an emoji). Ask, "What is this?" without identifying the emotion. See how the children respond. Then introduce a selected song that embodies that emotion. "How does this song feel to you?" Now ask the children to show you what the emotion looks like. "How does 'happy' look in your face and body? What do you do when you are happy?"

To see is a visual cue. To hear is an auditory cue. To feel is a tactile cue. Check out the following emotion examples you can use with your group:

- **Happy**

  Visual cue: show a picture of a happy face.

  Auditory cue: listen to a happy song like "Happy" (Williams 2013).

  Tactile cue: move in a happy way. "What does 'happy' look like in your body?"

- **Sad**

  Visual cue: show a picture of a sad face.

  Auditory cue: listen to sad music like "Running Out of Time" (Radin 2012). This is not classified as children's music, but it's a melancholy song and illustrates the many options available and appropriate for the classroom.

  Tactile cue: move or act as if you are sad.

- **Excited**

  Visual cue: show a picture of an excited face.

  Auditory cue: choose an upbeat sound, perhaps a jazz song like Duke Ellington's "Digga Digga Doo (Reprise)" (2011). Or try the Irish jig, "Tell Me Ma" (Gaelic Storm 1998). My three daughters participated in Irish dancing, so this song brings back happy memories for me.

  Tactile cue: move or act as if you are excited.

- **Tired/Sleepy**

  Visual cue: show a picture of a sleepy face.

  Auditory cue: listen to a musical selection such as "Binaural Beats" (Binaural Beats 2012).

  Tactile cue: lie down on the floor, close eyes, and rest.

ACTIVITY • Pick a Positive Movement Song

Listen to a positive song and include any actions that go along with the words in the song. I fell in love with a song by Vincent Nunes, "No One's Going to Keep Me Down" (2014), during a continuing education course with him. It's all about building strength and resilience.

Winding Down

End with cooldown activities by slowing the pace of your usual warm-up activities; this changes the children's focus to stretching and cooling down:

- Point and flex in long sit.

- Lift one leg straight up from long sit, then put it on the floor and lift the other leg.

- Be a roly-poly bug. Lie on your back with arms and legs in the air, and wiggle them.

- Perform cow and cat poses. Get on all fours with hands and knees on the floor. Drop your belly down to the floor while you raise your head to look up. Arch your back and look down toward your belly. Repeat a few times.

- Touch your nose to the floor. Kneel with your hands and knees on the floor, bend your elbows to bring your nose to the floor; straighten your elbows to push your body back up using your arms. Repeat.

- Roll. Lie flat on your back and roll your body from side to side like a log.

- Perform the rock pose. Lie on your back and hug your knees to your chest.

- Take-5 breathe. Breathe in for a count of five, then breathe out for a count of five.

- Sing a goodbye song (for example, see "Winding Down" in lesson 1 on page 28).

Lesson 36 *The Space around Us*

This lesson is helpful for children who sometimes bump into other children. Island hopping will be a challenge for these children, yet the game offers a safe practice structure. **Warning**: The final song in this lesson will "stick" in your head all day. (Pun intended!)

Supplies

- sitting spots
- paper plates
- hoops
- scarves
- music
- Hoberman sphere

Getting Started

Seat everyone in the opening circle. Place the Hoberman sphere in the middle. Talk about the personal pretend bubbles around us and what your personal space means. Open and close the Hoberman sphere to demonstrate the concepts of stretch and collapse. Tell the children to try to stretch their arms and legs like the sphere when it opens, and to collapse, bend forward, and become as small as they can when it closes. Repeat a few times. Move on to warm-up activities.

Warm-Up

- Stretch and shrink: Grow big and then small.
- Point and flex feet: Sit in a long sit, with legs in front.
- Ladybug, ladybug, get your toes: Make pincer fingers and hop them down your legs to your toes.
- Open and close legs: Sit with legs outstretched, move legs wide apart, and then close the space between them.

- Stomp feet: Sit with knees bent and feet on the floor. Tap feet on floor to make a loud sound. Then try to tap feet on the floor quietly. Alternate making loud and quiet stomps.

- Blow up balloons: Use breath and arms to grow big, opening arms wide.

- Fly like a bird: Lie on your belly, then fly like a bird by raising arms and legs briefly. Repeat.

- Grow bigger, bigger, and jump: Squat and slowly stand up as you say, "bigger," then jump upward with both feet.

ACTIVITY • Paper Plate Game

Each child in the circle gets a paper plate.

Say, "It's time to look and try. Can you touch your knee with the plate? Touch your head. Touch your nose. Can you touch your back?"

Name as many body parts as you can, touching the plate to each part and saying its name. Try to be specific, saying, "Elbow, shoulder, thumb, wrist, upper thigh, lower leg, big toe, abdomen."

ACTIVITY • Free Dancing

Time without instruction is freeing. This is especially true for children, since much of their day is directed by adults. Set a timer. Tell the group to observe their own space bubbles and to explore what they want to do with their scarves when they hear the music start. "When the music stops, please freeze and wait to hear about the next game."

ACTIVITY • Island Hopping

Music: go tropical!

Place hoops around the room on the floor.

Ask the children, "What is an island?" Affirm their responses with "a piece of land surrounded by water on all sides."

Tell them that each hoop will be an island. The space around the islands is water.

Demonstrate a flying action and say, "When the music starts, be a bird flying around the islands over the water and flapping your arms like wings. When the music stops, fly to an island and stand inside it or put at least one foot on the island. Please share the islands. Let's fit as many birds as we can on each island."

Start music. Fly around the hoops by flapping arms up and down. Stop music. Each child should find a hoop and stand inside it. Once all the children understand, remove one hoop during each flying session. They will start to realize that there are fewer islands on which to land and that they will need to cooperate with each other to figure out how they will all fit on an island. This introduces the math concept of subtraction.

Continue removing hoop islands until the least number are left that the children can manage to safely stand inside together.

Winding Down

"Icky Sticky Bubblegum" is a popular action song of unknown origin. Take a piece of pretend bubblegum. Pop it in your mouth. Chew it up and pop it out onto your hands. Rub or slide both of your palms together as you sing,

> *Icky sticky, sticky, sticky bubblegum, bubblegum, bubblegum.*
>
> *Icky sticky, sticky, sticky bubblegum, bubblegum, bubblegum.*
>
> *Makes your hands stick to your **knees**.* (Put hands on knees and pretend they are stuck.)
>
> *You pull them and you pull them and you pull them away!* (Final pull, hands are free.)

Repeat the song, replacing "knees" with various body parts:

- head
- belly
- mouth (this may not be the best choice during flu season)
- nose
- elbows

Warning: This song will be stuck in your head all day.

Chapter 10

APPENDIX A
Samplers and Transitions

Use the activities in this section when you need a new game to play and are short on time. You'll find ideas here on how to mesh movement with poetry and how to use rhyming words with actions. In addition, this section includes a few action songs you can sing, a basic qigong warm-up, fine-motor control tips, and a discussion of crossing midline activities.

Poetry in Motion

An adorable boy in my twins' preschool class kept in his pocket a poem that his parents had given him. He would take it out, unfold it, look at it, and put it back in his pocket. The words on that paper were special to him even if he couldn't read them. Perhaps the paper gave him comfort and reminded him of being with his parents while he was at school. Poetry is a great way to inspire a love of words in our children.

That said, I am not fond of poetry. But this little boy inspired me to try something new and get outside of my boxed thinking. Read a poem out loud to your children and make up movements to go along with the words. Try including whole-body position changes to stand up, sit down, or roll on the floor.

ACTIVITY • Pick a Poet

All you need to do is find a poem you love and figure out what types of body movements your children can do to accompany the words. One such poem is "When I Was a Baby" (Lansky 2000). It makes me smile every time I read it to a class because it talks about burping, a topic that surprises and captivates the children.

When you read the word *applauded* in this poem, have the children clap. The class can also stand up, sit down, and make happy or sad faces to mirror the corresponding words when they occur in the poem. When the mother in the poem "clucks," it's an opportunity to make a clicking sound with the tongue. Making this sound helps develop the control of oral muscles that are needed for speech and language acquisition.

You can modify any poem by adding movements or sounds like clicking the tongue. Here's another example of a poem and movements that can accompany it.

ACTIVITY • A Transition Poem (Source Unknown)

One for the mouse *(Stay low in a crawling position.)*
One for the crow *(Stand on tiptoes, with arms out to the sides like a bird.)*
One to stop *(Stand still and freeze.)*
One to go *(Jog in place, bringing knees up high.)*

ACTIVITY • Just Rhyme

An alternative to a poem is to break down a phrase or even two simple rhyming words. Use as a classroom transition or within a movement activity lesson plan. Here's how it's done.

Get a small- to medium-size red exercise ball, something a child can grab with two outstretched hands and with arms straight. Stand in a circle and pass the ball around the circle, keeping feet facing the center of the circle. Use two hands and twist the torso to pass to the person next to you.

Now say, "Round and round the red ball goes. Where it stops, nobody knows. One, two, three, four, five, *stop!*"

Challenge

Pass the ball to each other with arms over the head or behind the back.

Short and Sweet Action Songs

ACTIVITY • "Bicycle Legs"

Sing or listen to the song "I Have a Little Bicycle" (Sunseri 2001b) while lying on your back with legs and feet in the air. Make bicycling actions by moving arms in circles. Or pretend to pedal an upside-down bicycle by moving legs in circles in the air.

Placing your feet above your heart and head helps circulation. It surprises me every time I try this how effective it is as an aerobic activity. It will definitely increase your heart rate. Tell a little story to engage the children in this activity, something like this:

Okay. Hop onto your bike. Let's go for a ride.

Wave to your friend next door.

I see a stop sign straight ahead. Stop.

Now, cross the street.

Ruff, ruff. Do you hear what I hear? Ruff, ruff.

Oh, a noisy dog is loose. Better go faster. Pedal faster.

Whew, we made it. We're going up a hill.

Slow down; make big circles in the air. Big, long, slow pedaling.

We are at the top; put your legs out wide and coast down the hill.

We made it!

ACTIVITY • "We Can Jump"

Sing the following song, performing the actions at the same time.

We can jump, jump, jump.
We can hop, hop, hop.
We can clap, clap, clap.
We can stop, stop, stop.
We can shake our heads for yes.
We can shake our heads for no.
We can bend our knees a little bit
And sit down slow.

ACTIVITY • "Song for Crab Pose"

We are little orange crabs by the sea.
Playing on the sand, we're happy as can be.
Watch us crawling this way and that way, too,
And then go swimming in the sea so blue.

ACTIVITY • "Shake It"

Shake it, shake it, shake it,
shake it all you can;
shake it like a milkshake any way you can.
Rumble to the bottom, rumble to the top.
Turn around and turn around.
Until you make it stop.

Take It Slow: A Qigong Warm-Up

Awhile back, I discovered a book about qigong. Every morning, I performed the sequenced breathing and standing actions in it. It took all of ten minutes to complete. Stretch up to the sky, breathing in. Breathe in with arms out to the side. Breathe in, up on tiptoes. Breathe out. The sequences even included a quick breath out with a one-two punch into the air in front of me. I decided to try a few of the sequences with my classes. They took to it and especially loved to release energy by punching into the air.

You can try any activity and modify it for your students. You don't have to repeat it perfectly. Just enjoy it, and you may be surprised by how well the activity is received.

Fine-Motor Tips

Fine-motor development grows with practice and with exposure to various types of activities that use the fingers and hands for precise movements. Its positive developmental outcomes include increased coordination, improved perception, and spatial awareness. I could get more technical, but the bottom line is that the following activities help maximize motor and brain development.

Try a few fine-motor favorites:

- Pop tubes. These are bendable tubes that can be snapped together. Pull and push them together and apart.

- Put a small, lightweight ball in a pop tube and let it travel the length of the tube and come out the other end. Repeat.

- Pull a rope secured to the wall.

- Holding small crayons, trace and draw on paper.

- Dip the tops of clean nail polish brushes into water and "paint" on a blackboard.

- Draw with short markers to develop grip.

- Write with paper placed on a wedge, so that arms are resting in an elevated position.

- Cut paper with safety scissors.

- Try messy hand activities: play with foam, playdough, and shaving cream.

- Practice pulling tape off a table: attach tape to table and ask the child to remove it.

- Play with plastic tweezers.

- Squeeze eyedroppers to transfer water from one place to another.

- Play with tactile tables that have objects hidden in trays of rice; search for the objects.

- Crawl through tunnels.

- Play with strings and beads.

- Hold cards to play a card game.

- Paint on a wall easel.

- Involve children in preparing snack by asking each one to cut a banana with a child-safe plastic knife.

- Rip papers.

- Push laundry baskets across the room by gripping a basket's handle.

Exercise Your Brain

You can use information that is processed by multiple areas of the brain to exercise and develop your child's brain. Introducing crossing midline activities and performing motions that require active involvement of both sides of the body will enhance the learning process.

Many in the education field are familiar with Brain Gym (Dennison and Dennison 2010), described as simple activities for whole-brain learning. The founders of Brain Gym, Paul E. and Gail E. Dennison, call it *educational kinesiology*. The essence of their technique focuses on energy exercises, lengthening activities, and midline movements.

Paul Dennison was a teacher who realized in the 1970s that his students who were having trouble reading used one-sided movements. The Brain Gym method was developed to synchronize the whole system for effortless learning and performing—in other words, to coordinate both sides of the brain for more effective learning.

The idea to incorporate both sides of the brain was not new to early rehabilitation professionals. In physical therapy treatment, using both hemispheres of the brain is highlighted in the work of Herman Kabat, PhD, MD. In the 1950s, Kabat based his approach to rehabilitation on research in neurophysiology. He employed spiral and diagonal patterns of movement with muscle facilitation to achieve a desired outcome (Voss, Ionta, and Myers 1985).

Let's back up and review: the brain has two hemispheres. When an adult has a stroke on one side of the brain, it's the other side of the body that has weakness. This is just one type of stroke-induced brain injury, but it shows that nerve pathways cross from one side of the body to the other. Physical therapists use crossing-midline activities during nervous system recovery. Movement is not linear, which is why exercises with muscle groups are practiced in diagonal patterns as a technique to enhance neuromuscular recovery.

When children perform crossing-midline tasks, they extend an arm or leg across to the other side of their body. This diagonal movement across the body encourages nervous system development. Spontaneously crossing the midline is considered a developmental milestone, which is usually fully integrated by eight or nine years of age.

Ways to Implement Crossing the Midline

Reference *Brain Gym Teacher's Edition*, which shows techniques (Dennison and Dennison 2010). The suggestions below are some of my favorite ways to challenge the nerve pathways. They encourage a child to achieve the motor milestone of successfully using strategies to cross the middle of the body.

- **Elbow to opposite knee**: Place a sticker on the right hand or elbow and another sticker on the left knee. Ask the child to touch both stickers together. Then touch the nonstickered left arm and right knee together.

- **Pass the ball**: Stand or sit in a circle or on a bench. Reach from right to left as you pass the ball to the person next to you. The idea is to sit still and not move your body, only your arms.

- **Back-to-back pass**: Two children sit cross-legged with their backs touching. Maintaining their backs touching, one child passes the ball from his right side to his partner's left side. Repeat a few times.

- **Give yourself a hug**: With elbows in front of chest, reach hands toward opposite shoulders to form an X shape.

- **Draw an 8 in the air** (Dennison and Dennison 2010): In the air, trace the shape of the number 8. Try to make an 8 with each arm alone. Then do so with hands clasped together. Say, "Grab a pretend paintbrush with both hands and paint a big 8 in the air."

- **Draw an infinity symbol** (a sideways 8) on a blackboard so that your students can trace it in the air.

- **Crawling**: It may not involve crossing the midline, but the coordination needed to crawl involves an arm and a leg on opposite sides of the body moving forward together.

- **Trunk twists**: Seated or standing, let your arms hang down and twist or rotate your body from side to side.

Winding Down

Do you remember Mr. Rogers, the children's television show host from 1968 to 2001? He always sang the same song at the end of his show. It was his signature farewell, and we all knew it was time to go when we heard it.

Catch phrases and cute songs stay in your head. Marie Forleo is an internet business coach with a popular online vlog at www.marieforleo.com. At the end of each video, she closes with her own manifesto: "Keep going for your dreams." She says it every time, it doesn't seem to get old, and her audience keeps watching and growing.

You can probably think of several catchy tunes or phrases you use or hear every day. I find myself using my own daily closing phrase, which happened organically. The students took to it quickly; if I forget to say my closing, it never fails that the students will remind me to say it. They affirm the importance of a good closing phrase. Plus, we seem to be wired to hear such phrases.

"Thank you for coming to movement,
you never know what we're gonna do . . .
next time."

I say this simple statement every time the children leave my class, and at the pause, the class finishes the phrase by saying "next time" out loud. You can use your own ending phrase and make it a fun, predictable way to end your movement lessons.

On that ending note, please have fun implementing these ideas. Explore what works for you and your children. Revise or revisit lessons as needed. Invent new activities. Start by setting up a structure, yet be flexible. You've got this!

Sitting Warm-Ups

Bigger, bigger, jump: Squat with knees bent and bottom down but not touching the floor. Slowly straighten your knees as you say, "Bigger." End by jumping up using both feet.

Blow up a pretend balloon: Sit on the floor with knees bent in front of you. Hold a pretend balloon in your fingers, then use your breath to blow air into your hands. As you do so, start to stretch your arms out to the sides. Once your arms are fully outstretched, gently rock or "fall" onto your back with knees tucked into your chest.

Carousel: Sit with knees bent and feet on the floor in front of you. Use your hands and feet to turn around and around in a circle. Keep your bottom on the floor. This works best on a smooth surface.

Cat pose: Place knees and hands on the ground, then arch your back up like a cat while you look down at your belly.

Count down to toes: Sit in a long sit with legs straight out in front. Use hands to tap your legs from your upper thigh down to your toes. Count as you tap. Try saying numbers in different languages.

Cow pose: Place knees and hands on the ground, drop your belly toward the floor, and look up. Moo like a cow.

Crab lifts: Sit with knees bent in front and feet on the floor in front of you. Place your hands behind you with palms on the floor. Now lift your bottom off the floor. Hold for a few seconds. Drop your bottom back down to the floor. Repeat. (Extending arms and fingers in front of you stretches the shoulders, but extending them behind you, as in this activity, stretches the shoulders even more.)

Downward-facing dog pose: Facing downward, place hands and feet on the floor. Space them far enough apart to allow your bottom to lift into the air. Your body should create a V shape. Hang your head between your arms. Heels can be lifted or touching the floor.

Hand walk: This is a pre-plank pose. Start by kneeling with hands and knees on the floor. Walk your hands away from your knees, then slowly walk them back. Repeat.

Hiss like a snake: Lie on your belly and lift your head up without using your arms or forearms, which will extend your back. Make a hissing sound.

Ladybug, ladybug, get your toes: Sit in a long sit with legs straight out in front. Use pincer-grip fingers and make little hand-hops from your upper thighs all the way down to touch your toes. For each hop, say, "Ladybug, ladybug, touch your toes."

Make a PB&J sandwich: Sit with legs open wide in a V shape. The space in front of you between your legs is your pretend table. Reach behind you and, one by one, grab the pretend ingredients you need for your sandwich. Now, use your hands to make the sandwich in front of you on your "table," saying the actions as you do so. Don't forget to squash and cut your sandwich in a manner that produces an inner thigh stretch.

Open and close your legs: Sit in a long sit with legs touching each other. Open the legs to make a V shape, then close them. Say "open" and "close" a few times as you move your legs accordingly. Say these words both slowly and quickly.

Point and flex your toes: Sitting with legs stretched out in front, move your ankles to point your toes away from you. Bend your ankles to bring the toes toward you.

Seated leg kicks: Sit with knees bent and feet on the floor in front of you. Lift and straighten one leg in front of you. Keep it straight while you place it back down on the floor. Repeat with the other leg. Then simultaneously lift both legs into a V position with both feet in the air. Your abdominal muscles will be working to keep you balanced on your bottom. Hold briefly. For extra fun, sing "Ahh!" while you do this.

Seed to flower: Curl your body into a ball on the floor. Describe how the seed is surrounded by dirt and that a gentle rain is falling. The sun comes out and warms the seed. Slowly lift a finger, then a hand, then an arm upward away from your body. Then lift the other arm incrementally. Slowly stand up and stretch your "petals" (arms and hands) to the sun.

Shake it high, shake it low: Using a high voice, say, "High," as your arms are stretched way above your head and your hands wiggle in the air. Then use a low voice and say, "Low," as you wiggle your hands down at your sides.

Stomp it out, loud and soft: Sit with knees bent and feet on the floor in front of you. It's best to have shoes on. Alternating knees, lift them up and down to stomp your feet on the floor. Stomp loudly. Then say, "Shhh," and alternate knees while tapping your feet quietly. Repeat, alternating loud and soft tapping.

Take-5 breathe: Sit or stand. Inhale deeply for a count of five seconds. If you choose, you can count on your fingers and show one finger for each breath. Then exhale for a count of five seconds. Repeat three times.

Wake up body: Gently tap or touch your neck, shoulders, arms, and legs.

Standing Warm-Ups

Arm circles: Stretch your arms out to the sides. Make small circles in the air with your arms until you can feel the effort of the muscles in your arm.

Elbow to knee: Touch your right elbow to your left knee. If your children don't know right from left, demonstrate it while you stand next to them, or place stickers on the opposite limbs that will touch. Repeat.

Figure eights: Clasp your hands together and pretend to draw a large number 8 in the air in front of you. Be sure to use your trunk and arms when "drawing." A picture of an 8 nearby can serve as a visual cue.

Gentle side twists: Gently shake out tension in your arms. Then turn and twist your body so that your arms swing from side to side.

Paint a rainbow in the air: Clasp your hands together and dip them into a pretend bucket of paint on one side of your body. Keep your feet in place on the floor. Reach up with your clasped hands and make an arch over your head to the other side of your body. Each time you reach up and over from one side to the other, call out a color of the rainbow that you are "painting."

Side stretches: Reach hands up and over your head. Now reach a little to one side with arms still up. With arms still up, try to reach hands up and over to the other side.

Sweep arms up to the sky: Stand with feet parallel and touching each other. Lift your arms up above your head, reaching as high as you can.

Sweep the floor: Touch your toes. Gently move your arms from side to side like you are sweeping the floor with your fingers.

Tiptoes up and down: Try to lift your heels up off the floor so that you are on tiptoes. Say "Up" and "Down" as you do this. Repeat a few times.

Touch toes: Reach down to touch your toes with your hands, keeping knees straight. Stay in that position for a few seconds. Remember, bottoms stay in the air. Some children will want to bend their knees. Say, "Try to keep your knees as straight as they can be."

Songs

Asher, James. 2002. "Red Rhythm Dragon." Track 3 on *Shaman Drums*. Starfield, compact disc.

Binaural Beats. 2012. "Healing Sleep Music." *Binaural Beats*. Independent Artist, digital music.

BusSongs.com. 2017. "Row Row Row Your Boat." Accessed October 16. www.bus-songs.com/songs/row-row-row-your-boat.

Damast, Deborah, and Sarah Lavan. 2003. *Move 'N Groove Kids, Vol. 1*. Directed by Manny Kivowitz. New York: KSK Studios, DVD.

Ellington, Duke, vocalist and instrumentalist. 2011. "Digga Digga Do (Reprise)." Track 8 on *Rug Cutter*. Cool Note, digital music. Originally released as "Diga Diga Do" in 1928.

Gaelic Storm. 1998. "Tell Me Ma." Track 6 on *Gaelic Storm*. Higher Octave Music, compact disc.

Gara, Kataka, instrumentalist. 2009. "Dragonfly Hang (Live at Steel Feel)." Track 10 on *Songs of Life*, Temple of Perfection, compact disc.

Greg and Steve, vocalists and instrumentalists. 1987. "Animal Action 1." Track 3 on *Kids in Motion*. Greg and Steve Productions, compact disc.

———. 2000. "Goin' on a Bear Hunt." Track 4 on *Kids in Action*. Greg and Steve Productions, compact disc.

Hartmann, Jack, vocalist and instrumentalist. 2010. "Penguin Dance Chant." Track 2 on *Get On Board the Transition Train (Transition Songs That Teach)*. Jack Hartmann, compact disc.

The Hit Crew Kids, vocalists. 2013. "Chicken Dance." By Terry Rendall and Werner Thomas. Track 11 on *Kids Dance Party Hits*. Drew's Famous, compact disc.

Johnny, vocalist and instrumentalist. 2003. "Balloon Song" on *Kids are Great!* John G/Johnny, compact disc.

Johnny Only, vocalist and instrumentalist. 2012. "Tootie Ta (Tooty Tot)." Single.

Karma Kids Yoga. 2008. "Rub Your Hands (Om Song)." Track 1 on *Come Play Yoga!* CD Baby, compact disc.

Martin, Dean, vocalist. 1966. "Let It Snow, Let It Snow, Let It Snow." By Sammy Cahn and Jule Styne. Track 5 on *The Dean Martin Christmas Album*. Reprise Records, 33⅓ rpm.

Namaste Kid. 2012. *Once upon A Mat*. Golden Valley, MN: Namaste Kid, DVD.

Nunes, Vincent, vocalist. 2014. "No One's Going to Keep Me Down." Track 2 on *Smart Songs for Active Children*. Lighthouse Records, compact disc.

Playful Planet. 2010. *Storyland Yoga*. Los Osos, CA: Playful Planet, DVD.

"Popcorn." 2007. *Popcorn*. Big Eye Records, digital.

Radin, Joshua, vocalist and instrumentalist. 2012. "Running Out of Time." Track 14 on *Underwater*. So Recordings, digital music.

Raffi, vocalist and instrumentalist. 1996. "Shake My Sillies Out." Track 13 on Disc 2 of *The Singable Songs Collection*. Rounder, digital music.

Soloway, Mike, vocalist and instrumentalist. 2013. "Animal Rap." Track 2 on *Preschool Action Songs 1*, digital music.

Sunseri, MaryLee, vocalist and instrumentalist. 2001a. "Head and Shoulders." Track 5 on *1,2,3 Sing with Me!* Piper Grove Music, compact disc.

———. 2001b. "I Have a Little Bicycle." Track 4 on *1,2,3—Sing with Me!* Piper Grove Music, compact disc.

———. 2001c. "The Wheels on the Bus." Track 20 on *1,2,3—Sing with Me!* Piper Grove Music, compact disc.

They Might Be Giants. 2005. "Clap Your Hands." Track 24 on *They Might Be Giants: Here Come the ABCs*. Walt Disney Records, compact disc.

Ultimate Camp Resource. 2018. "Camp Songs." Accessed July 12. www.ultimatecampresource.com/site/camp-activities/camp-songs.html.

Van Dyke, Dick, Julie Andrews, Karen Dotrice, and Matthew Garber, vocalists. 1997. "Chim Chim Cher-ee." Written by Robert B. Sherman and Richard M. Sherman. Recorded 1964. Track 14 on *Mary Poppins Original Soundtrack*. Walt Disney Records, digital music.

Wenig, Marsha. 2003. *YogaKids: Silly to Calm*. Directed by Ted Landon. Louisville, CO: Gaiam, DVD.

Williams, Pharrell, vocalist. 2013. "Happy." Track 4 on *Despicable Me 2 (Original Motion Picture Soundtrack)*. Back Lot Music, compact disc.

References

AAOS (American Academy of Orthopaedic Surgeons). 2006. "Position Statement: Children and Musculoskeletal Health." Last modified September 2016. www .aaos.org/uploadedFiles/PreProduction/About/Opinion_Statements /position/1170%20Children%20and%20Musculoskeletal%20Health.pdf.

APTA (American Physical Therapy Association). 2013. "Vision Statement for the Physical Therapy Profession and Guiding Principles to Achieve the Vision." Last modified March 20, 2018. www.apta.org/Vision/.

———. 2018. "Movement System." APTA. Accessed June 7. www.apta.org /MovementSystem.

Dennison, Paul E., and Gail E. Dennison. 2010. *Brain Gym® Teacher's Edition*. Ventura, CA: Edu-Kinesthetics.

Dow, Connie Bergstein. 2006. *Dance, Turn, Hop, Learn! Enriching Movement Activities for Preschoolers*. St. Paul, MN: Redleaf Press.

Duhigg, Charles. 2014. *The Power of Habit: Why We Do What We Do in Life and Business*. New York: Random House.

Kids Yoga Stories. 2016. "10 Autumn Yoga Poses for Kids." www.kidsyogastories.com /autumn-yoga.

Kranowitz, Carol, and Joye Newman. 2010. *Growing an In-Sync Child: Simple and Fun Activities to Help Every Child Develop, Learn and Grow*. New York: Penguin.

Lansky, Bruce. 2000. *If Pigs Could Fly . . . and Other Deep Thoughts*. Minnetonka, MN: Meadowbrook Press.

Lasater, Judith Hanson, and Ike K. Lasater. 2009. *What We Say Matters: Practicing Nonviolent Communication*. Berkeley, CA: Rodmell Press.

Mullett, Sara. 2013. "How to Tell the Difference between the Rhythm & the Beat." *Let's Play Music*. www.letsplaykidsmusic.com/rhythm-and-beat.

NAEYC (National Association for the Education of Young Children). 2009. "NAEYC Standards for Early Childhood Professional Preparation." https://www.naeyc .org/sites/default/files/globally-shared/ downloads/PDFs/resources /position-statements/2009%20Professional%20Prep%20stdsRevised%204 _12.pdf.

National Institute for Early Education Research (NIEER). 2017a. *State of Preschool 2016*. http://nieer.org/state-preschool-yearbooks/yearbook2016.

———. 2017b. "Press Release: New Research Reveals Growing Inequality among States in Access to High-Quality Public Preschool." http://nieer.org/wp-content /uploads/2017/05/YB2016_Montana.pdf.

Pica, Rae. 2003. *Your Active Child: How to Boost Physical, Emotional, and Cognitive Development through Age-Appropriate Activity*. New York: McGraw-Hill.

Revermann, Susan. 2017. "How to Determine the Right Jump Rope Size for Kids." *How to (Adult)*. Last modified September 26, 2017. http://howtoadult.com /determine-right-jump-rope-size-kids-25503.html.

Riggs, Maida L., ed. 1980. *Movement Education for Preschool Children*. Reston, VA: American Alliance for Health, Physical Education, Recreation and Dance. www .eric.ed.gov/contentdelivery/servlet/ERICServlet?accno=ED204303.

Scott, S. J. 2017. *Habit Stacking: 127 Small Changes to Improve Your Health, Wealth, and Happiness*. Mahwah, NJ: Oldtown Publishing.

Stiffelman, Susan. 2012. *Parenting without Power Struggles*. New York: Atria Books.

Study.com. 2017. "Preschool Teacher Requirements and Career Information." Accessed September 17. http://study.com/preschool_teacher_requirements.html.

Thelen, Esther. 1995. "Motor Development: A New Synthesis." *American Psychologist* 50 (2): 79–95.

Vargas, Elizabeth. 2017. "Digital Addiction?" May 19, 2017. *20/20*. ABC.

Voss, Dorothy E., Marjorie K. Ionta, and Beverly J. Myers. 1985. *Proprioceptive Neuromuscular Facilitation: Patterns and Techniques*. 3rd ed. Philadelphia: Harper and Row.